NETWORK YOUR WAY TO ENDLESS ROMANCE

Media Contact:
ANNIE JENNINGS, PR
908.281.6201
Fax 908.281.5221

What People Are Saying About *Network Your Way To Endless Romance*

Network Your Way To Endless Romance is a great resource for anyone driven homicidal by the wrong relationships. Bob Burg shows how networking will do more than help us find people to date – it will help us find the right people to date.

– **Sandra Beckwith,**
author of *Why Can't A Man Be More Like A Woman?*

You've got to find a mate before you start to use romance to keep your mate! Bob Burg is an expert at the beginning stages of creating great relationships. I wish I'd known his networking techniques back when I was single!

– **Gregory J.P. Godek,**
author of *1001 Ways To Be Romantic*

It's a systematic and organized business-like approach to finding the mate of your dreams; it may not seem romantic, but it works!

– **Terri Murphy,**
author of *Listing & Selling Secrets*

I find *Network Your Way To Endless Romance* to be the textbook got dating in the nineties!

– **Mayriah Moore,**
author of *My, My, My...Dating in the '90s*
and dating expert featured on the USA Network

NETWORK YOUR WAY TO ENDLESS ROMANCE

Secrets to Help You Meet the Mate of Your Dreams

Bob Burg
with Laurie Sue Brockway

SAMARK PUBLISHING, INC.
JUPITER, FLORIDA

Copyright © 1997 by Bob Burg

All rights reserved. No part of this book may be reproduced or transmitted in any form or by any means, electronic or mechanical, including photocopying, recording or by any information storage and retrieval system, without permission in writing from the publisher.

The Romantic Resumé portion of this book is © 1997 Laurie Sue Brockway.

♥ Published by Samark Publishing, Inc.
725 North A1A, Suite E109, Jupiter, Florida 33477

Publisher's Cataloging-in-Publication Data
Burg, Bob.
   Network your way to endless romance : secrets to help you meet the mate of your dreams / Bob Burg with Laurie Sue Brockway—Jupiter, Florida : Samark Publishing, Inc., c1997.
     p. cm.
   Includes biographical references and index.
   ISBN: 0-9650285-1-8
   1. Mate selection. 2. Dating (social customs). 3. Man-woman relationships. I. Brockway, Laurie Sue. II. Title. III. Title: Endless romance.
HQ801.B87   1996
306.7'3–dc20   95-94808

PROJECT COORDINATED BY JENKINS GROUP

99 98 97 ❖ 5 4 3 2 1

Printed in the United States of America

To Mom and Dad

It's been said that the greatest gift parents can possibly give their children is to love each other. Your marriage is a shining example of how the right partnership can provide a lifetime of joy and bring out the best life has to offer. I love you!

– Bob

PREMISE

This book is designed to show you how to take a uniquely business-like approach to fulfilling the very human desire to love and be loved.

The intent is to guide you, step by step, toward meeting the mate of your dreams óor reaching whatever level of dating activity and success you may desire.

In many ways, these techniques and insights are quite simple: They illustrate how to apply business networking skills to finding romance; and how to cultivate new friendships that will help make dreams come true. Along the way you will follow your own heart, employ common sense and utilize a little old-fashioned ingenuity to transform your love life.

If you, like so many others, were raised with the notion "someday my prince (princess) will come," the concept of "networking" for love may seem strange. However, this is a safe and exciting way to meet new people, and it is *guaranteed* to increase your odds of meeting the *right* people, and, ultimately, the right person for *you*.

If you have preconceived notions regarding the term "networking," you are encouraged to lay them aside, because, in the context of this book, you will come to see the term networking in a whole new light.

If you are already a naturally giving person who likes to do things for others, and who would welcome the chance to expand your life by expanding your circle of friends and acquaintances, read on, and discover how you can *Network Your Way To Endless Romance*.

CONTENTS

Premise..7
Acknowledgments..13
Introduction...17

Part One
First Stop: The Romantic Resumé......................................27
The first step to romantic success is to clarify your goals. The Romantic Resumé Questionnaire is the starting point of your dating adventures and it will assist you throughout your journey of finding a mate. Learn how to construct a Romantic Resumé based on what you discover while filling out the questionnaire.

Part Two
Everything You Need To Know About Networking Your Way To Endless Romance..61
A step-by step system for mastering the art of networking that will teach you sure-fire techniques for networking success, and guide you through what to do and say to transform your love life.

Chapter 1 *What Is Networking, Anyway?*........................63
A primer on the principles of powerful networking that will expand your definition of "networking" and bring your many romantic options to life.

Chapter 2 *Referral-Based Dating: A New Trend In Romance*..75
The proverbial blind date grows up as people learn to effectively "connect" their friends. Learn the *proactive* and *reactive* approaches to "Referral-Based Dating," the power meeting of the '90s.

Chapter 3 *Follow The Golden Rule To Endless Romance* 85
Great things come to nice people. This simple philosophy is the most effective foundation for building a network and creating a huge, flourishing support system of friends and acquaintances.

Chapter 4 *Networking Is For The Shy* 95
Use shyness to your advantage. How shy, reserved and quiet types of people can use networking to build confidence and communication skills.

Chapter 5 *Looking For Love In All The Right Places* 105
Tips, techniques and ideas for expanding your options for meeting new people. Once you clarify the types of people you want to meet, learn how to set about meeting them on common ground.

Chapter 6 *Networking Step-by-Step* 115
A sure-fire system for meeting new people and winning them over. These no-fail techniques show how to communicate with new people in ways that will make them want to know you, like you and trust you. Learn to ask all the right questions.

Chapter 7 *Continue To Make An Impression* 143
Follow-up that will ensure your new contacts remember who you are. Discover several seldom-used, yet simple, techniques that will keep you forever on a person's mind.

Chapter 8 *Putting Your Plan Into Action* 157
Make sure your contacts think of you when the "right person" comes along. Now that you've got their attention, get their support in finding that special someone. Learn a series of techniques and questions that will help you in your quest for love.

Chapter 9 *Taking Control Of Your Destiny* *165*
Turn your romantic project into adventure and fun. Actively work with networking friends to achieve your goals using no-fail methods for meeting many new people. Learn the effective ways people have networked for endless romance.

Part Three
Avoiding "Relationship Malpractice" *175*

Chapter 10 *The Anatomy of Referral-Based Romance*..*177*
Tips from Laurie Sue on how to use the dating process to further clarify romantic goals and select the right person as the mate of your dreams.

Chapter 11 *Effective Communication Is The Key to Endless Romance*..*189*
Strategies and insights that will help you avoid "Relationship Malpractice" by nourishing your relationship with clear, caring communication.

Part Four
Your Continued Success *209*

Chapter 12 *Keep Yourself On Track* *211*
Follow The Roadmap for Success toward a lifetime of relationship fitness and success in all areas of life!

Glossary of Terms *221*
About the Authors *224*
Resource Guide *227*
Index *233*

ACKNOWLEDGMENTS

From Bob:

No book reflects the work of one lone author, and this book especially is an extraordinary collaborative effort. So many people contributed ideas, writing, editing, correcting, proofreading, production and more, that I get tired just *thinking* of the effort it would've taken to create this on my own. It also makes me appreciate all the great friends and associates I'm blessed with: wonderful people who care enough to put themselves out for me, and for you, the reader. Instead of thanking *everyone,* which would take up far too many pages, let me thank just a handful of people who went above and beyond and made many significant and transformational contributions.

First, I want to acknowledge my dynamic and talented collaborator, Laurie Sue Brockway for the insights, expertise and enthusiasm she brings to this book. Without her contribution and spirit, this would have been a very different project. Her personal experience and professional wisdom make her an extraordinarily well-informed source on dating and mating dynamics between men and women. Aside from being a top reporter and outstanding writer, she is a great relationship coach who truly wants people to make their romantic dreams come true.

I also want to thank Karen Wilkening, editor of the original *Endless Romance* manuscript. She's so great at what she does, she even makes *me* look like I know how to write! Mark, Alex, Cindy and the crew at the Jenkins Group, real professionals who have come through for me every time. Greg, a true modern entrepreneur and great guy, thanks for the much-needed advice.

Robert Smith, the business manager of one of my fellow speakers and authors: thank you for your unselfish help and advice over the past few years. Everyone should have a Robert Smith to manage their career. The contributors whose stories are featured throughout the pages of this book – WOW! – Thank you so much.

My office staff, who give 110% every day and help make my speaking habit possible by keeping me constantly on the road (actually, that's probably where they like me best!). I am so fortunate to have such a loyal, loving, and supportive crew.

And Cindy, my dear friend, who is so giving to everyone and does so much for me that I wonder how I can ever express my true appreciation.

And, of course, my family: my brother Rich; my sister and brother-in-law, Robyn & Steve; and their children, my gorgeous, baseball star niece, Samantha, and nephew, "Rhino" Mark. Sami and Mark, you two give me inspiration and joy every time I look at your pictures on my desk.

My family is headed by a most inspiring example of all that is good in my life: my parents, Mike and Myrna Burg. You are the ones who have *always* been on my side. My most vocal cheerleaders, biggest encouragers, and best friends. I love you more than mere words could ever possibly describe.

A special acknowledgment also goes to you, the reader. By virtue of your participation, feedback and networking success, you will help change the way that men and women meet, date and settle down. You will help carve out a new path toward love and *Endless Romance* – as you walk it yourself!

– Bob Burg

From Laurie Sue:

First, I want to thank Bob Burg for inviting me to join him in bringing his great networking techniques to life and in merging our male and female points of view! I acknowledge him with appreciation for approaching this project in the true spirit of cocreation. Bob has a contagious belief in the goodness of human beings and The Golden Rule. He's a powerhouse of expertise and know-how, *and* he is totally open to new perspectives. He also happens to be a true gentleman, who honors, respects and champions women's rights. It has been a great adventure!

This entire project has been an extraordinary tribute to the true power and possibilities of networking! The amazing Annie Jennings of Annie Jennings, PR, deserves kudos for bringing Bob and me together; and my pal Paul Scott Adamo of The Learning Annex in New York gets credit for introducing me to Annie.

I'd like to acknowledge Jennifer Reut, for copyediting and editorial guidance. Theodore A. Hagg, whose personal and professional support has touched my life deeply for 14 years. And Caroline Landau, for her unconditional friendship and support. Thanks also to Richard Kasak of Masquerade Books, who gave me my start as an author, and all my buddies over at *Playgirl* for giving me an enduring opportunity to learn ever more about human nature, sexuality and relationships. Of course, I cannot forget my soul sister scribes Patricia Kennealy-Morrison and Susan Crain Bakos – we authors with three names stick together!

I've got to thank the folks who gave me my primary experiences with love and the human heart: My Mom, Shirley Brockway, gets a big hug for raising me to be a strong and independent woman, and yet always being the shoulder I could cry on. My Dad, Lee Brockway, for teaching me some of the most important relationship lessons of my life. My big sisters Rikki and Nikki, whom I adore, for our deeply shared bonds of love and hereditary sense of humor. I must also thank my dear, sweet son, Alexander Kent, for teaching me what unconditional love *really means*, and continually challenging my heart to open and grow. Finally, I thank my partner in parenting, John Garrett; though we are no longer partners in life, together we're raising an amazing child who embodies the best of us both.

I'd be remiss if I did not acknowledge these very dear and special friends and teachers who have championed my understanding of love relationships, as well as my well-being: Dr. Rose McAloon, Rev. Barbara Glabman-Cohen, Dr. Ken Kafka, Dr. Judith Orloff, Dr. Judy Kuriansky, Lexie and Robert Potamkin, Merna Popper, Pat Rodegast, Emmanuel, and my Monday and Wednesday women's groups. Thank you to the great friends, media buddies and "civilians" who have allowed me to peer into their lives and tell their stories in print – here, and everywhere – over the past two decades. It has truly been an honor.

I dedicate my work in this book to all the women and men who will follow this magnificent game plan and make their romantic dreams come true...and to my own dream mate, Dr. Wonderful, who is getting closer by the day, by the moment.

– Laurie Sue Brockway

INTRODUCTION

A *Business-like* Approach To Meeting Your Mate?

The reason we wrote this book is quite simple – there is a need. And according to the people I meet when I travel and the newspaper and magazine articles I read, that need is HUGE. Terrific people like you complain constantly that they are mateless and dateless – and *clueless* about how to remedy the situation. I'm talking about attractive, bright, personable people – men and women alike. The question is: Why on earth can't these attractive, bright, personable men and women get together? Answer: Because until this book, those people were floundering around without a proven method to help them find one another. We hope that *Network Your Way To Endless Romance* is the road map that will help them find each other.

There may be a wide gulf between simply being dateless on Saturday night and desperate loneliness, but I believe the majority of single people find themselves somewhere in between. They are too busy to allow themselves to feel the strains of loneliness, yet they are yearning for a more significant connection in their lives.

It's not that they don't meet people – we *all* meet people, wherever we go – but many singles complain that the people they *do* meet are often people they'd rather not know. They aren't nice enough, or sane enough, or they are simply inappropriate matches. I can't even count the hundreds of people who have told both Laurie Sue and me that they often meet people with whom they have no chemistry, or with whom they do feel sexual chemistry but find no substance behind it.

It seems that some extremely wonderful people are falling through the cracks of the dating world. As a result, these wonderful people can end up settling for a mate who is not *exactly* right but who *is* there, and physically available. I'm not saying they settle because they're desperate, but I'd bet there are a lot of people who do settle because they are afraid they might *become* desperate. Many people feel that the high divorce rate in this country is partly due to couples that bail out of marriage all-too-easily. That thought is valid, but did you ever consider that maybe, just *maybe,* too many people are totally incompatible in the first place? Sometimes people simply do not give themselves enough "courting options."

A big challenge in the mating game today is time – or lack of it. Between work and family, obligations and errands, people are often wrung out by the end of the week, or just too busy to fit in anything else. If you're a divorced or a single parent, there's little time, energy or even desire to grapple with the so-called "dating scene."

Let's face it, folks: The "dating scene" in the nineties has become something of a "danger scene." These days, meeting people in the usual places, such as singles bars and nightclubs, is not only what I call "quality inefficient," it can be downright scary! It's not just the fear of a reprise of *Looking For Mr. Goodbar* (or Ms. Goodbar), or even the frightening prospect of catching a sexually transmitted disease: It's the simple fact that when you meet people out in a bar setting, you are meeting the person they are in bars. You know little about who they are, or what they're about, and the entire experience is colored by the fact that one or both of you have been drinking. It's an all-too-common experience to fall head over heels in *lust* with someone who looked really good on that bar stool, only to find, in the light of day, that you two had nothing to talk about.

The problem with some of the traditional ways people meet one another is that there is an inherently "short screening process," and the conditions for it are less than optimum. *There's just no way to get to know someone before engaging in the ritual of getting to know them.* For most adults, it takes more than a glance across a room, a brief meeting and a follow-up telephone conversation to tell where a person's head and heart are really at! (Hey, don't feel bad – remember 50 percent of the people who marry often *"don't"* figure it out until after they've said "I *do!*")

It may seem that the biggest risks are: 1) The possibility of wasting an evening with a person you may not like once you get to know him/her, or 2) That person turns out to be too clingy, possessive, talkative, silent, stoned, sexually incompatible, neurotic, psychotic, boring, etc. But it is more complex than that. Not only did you waste precious, valuable time with someone inappropriate, you shared a little part of yourself with an individual who did not honor or appreciate *you*. You gave something of yourself – even it was just over coffee – to someone who depleted your energy. Obviously, if you walk away from enough experiences feeling drained, you begin to lose hope and adopt the *belief* that dating is a draining experience.

My friend Susan once embarked on a dating experiment, going out with anyone who asked her. She wasn't sure what she was looking for, so she looked at everyone. Susan figured out what she wanted in a mate by experiencing all the things she did *not* want. After an exhausting series of dates, she decided she'd met enough "bad news" guys to last a lifetime; she'd done enough "research."

"Through the process of elimination, I crystallized my vision of the perfect mate," she recalls. "It gave me a chance to look into the dating market, and I found that, when I dated a number of people I didn't know well, I felt very vulnerable – my ego was really on the line. I sometimes wished I had a publicist who explained who I was and what I looked like before I got there, so I didn't have to keep repeating myself to so many guys. I learned a lot, so I am glad I did it. But it's not a process I would repeat again. At this time in my life, I really can't afford to diddle around with guys who don't share the same vision in life."

Now YOU are the one holding this book in your hands, so I'm going to assume you're looking for someone who is a good person with the potential to be in a healthy, happy, mature relationship – either short or long-term. You invested your money in this book, so I know you're willing to invest your resources in moving forward and finding more appropriate and efficient ways to meet quality people. And since you are obviously willing to make an effort toward achieving these goals, you must be ready to date the right people. That's why I'm going to teach you a proven system for becoming more "quality-efficient" in your dating practices and choices, and that means finding the people who possess the qualities you feel are desirable.

First, you've got to figure out your preferences in a potential date or mate. The Romantic ResumÈ Questionnaire, in Part One, will help pave the way. It is designed to help you clarify your relationship goals, to put on paper those things you're searching for in a mate and also to recognize what *you* are bringing to the party!

This is *not* a quiz – there are no right or wrong answers – and your personal tastes are all that matter. The point is: Until you *know* what you want, it's possible that anyone and everyone will appear desirable. It's important that you feel open-minded and ready for love, but you need to create structure and set some boundaries. You have to define what love means to you personally, and learn to look at your own value system. The dating horror stories that have been chapters in your life can serve to teach you what you *do not wish* to recreate; as you sort through past experiences with the wrong people, you can begin to assemble a new "wish list" of qualities you now seek in a date or mate-to-be.

This process will point you in the direction of connecting with more like-minded souls: people who are on the same wave-length, speak the same love language, and get your jokes! In Part Two, we'll go through the step-by-step program for utilizing business networking skills to expand social and romantic opportunities. Part Three will guide you through the dating process and pilot you toward a lifetime of loving.

The most successful marriages and long-term relationships result from strong friendships. True friendships develop between people who share a commonalty of interests: a similarity of ideas, values, views, and goals. Sure, it's been said that "opposites attract" – and they do – but the odds are that the opposite's attraction will eventually lose its novelty. Unless there is significant substance, understanding and communication, those attractions rarely last, and if they do, they often turn unpleasant! Once the honeymoon period wears off, the attraction will probably wear off as well. Lasting, successful, happy relationships that develop from love at first sight are rare. If you are someone who enjoys the drama and constant negotiation of trying to have a lover who sees life very differently than you, then so be it – but it can be very draining and ultimately unsatisfying. If you want a more harmonious and healthy union, you need to consider someone with similar values, life goals, and level of commitment.

So why is the myth of the great "opposite attraction" so pervasive? Maybe – (cue soap opera music) *because it provides a glimmer of hope that true romantics can cling to until they one day find it and live in ecstasy...*or it's the stuff from which great movies like *The Way We Were* and *Gone With The Wind* are made. But try living your whole life with someone who says "black" when you say "white," sees the glass half-empty when you see it half-full, or who just plain thrives on being adversarial. You'll either pull your hair out trying to change them, significantly diminishing your ideals to accommodate that other person's viewpoint – and thus losing an important part of yourself – or you'll become so conscious of the differences between you that you'll live in a perpetual state of anxiety and dissatisfaction. (Okay, you can cut the soap opera music now!)

One of the goals of this book is to help you significantly improve your chances of meeting your *second* husband or wife *first* – the type of person you can be friends with and with whom you can communicate honestly and openly. That may require you to become more focused about how you spend your time and with whom you associate.

You may think that this perspective seems calculating and unromantic – and you're right. But remember that many of life's most satisfying and joyful moments arrive after some of life's most unglamorous and agonizing processes. That's why, *this* time, you're going to attack romance in a business-like fashion – so that you don't live through any more dates that want to make you run away screaming! Relationships can be a difficult and confusing topic, but please keep in mind this new process can also be fun and enlightening and filled with revelations. Have an epiphany on us!

Conclusion/Important Thought

So we've established that it's easier to have a happy, rich and fulfilling relationship with someone who already has many of the attributes you desire in a mate than it is to try and change that person after the relationship is already underway.

Now, I can't guarantee you that everyone you meet will possess all the qualities you're looking for, or that you'll never, ever, go out on another bad date. Absolutely not! But I *can* guarantee that you'll significantly increase your chances of finding someone who's right for you.

Your mission, should you choose to accept it, is:
1) Define clearly what it is you are looking for in a date and a mate.
2) Meet and date as many new people of quality as you choose.
3) Have dating experiences that are more positive, powerful and productive.
4) Dramatically increase the odds that those individuals you *do* choose to be a part of your life will be of the highest quality possible and most able to make you happy.
5) Link up with your lifetime mate, if you so desire.
6) Network Your Way To Endless Romance – and help the others in your expanding network do the same!

Bob Burg
Jupiter, Florida

NETWORK YOUR WAY TO ENDLESS ROMANCE

PART ONE

♥

*First Stop On Your
Road To Romance:*

THE *R*OMANTIC RESUMÉ

You are about to embark on a magnificent adventure in search of your ideal date, and ultimately, your ideal mate. Naturally, you'd like to arrive at your destination with as few delays as possible. That's why your first stop should be putting together your personal Romantic Resumé. It's not a chronological account of your past relationships – although what didn't work in the past is a great guide for what you don't want to re-create in the future. Rather, it's an outline you can use to gain focus about the kind of person who would be your ideal match while creating a document that will put your dreams on paper. Your Romantic Resumé is a tool for turning romantic fantasies into reality.

I

Preparing Your Romantic Resumé

Why A Resumé For Romance?

Anyone can network their way to endless romance and the steps in this book will show you exactly how to proceed. But before you begin to follow the road map that will lead you to your destination, it's important that you know exactly where you desire to go. The intention of this portion of the *Network Your Way To Endless Romance* system is to help you do a reality check on your fantasies, crystallize your desires and preferences and create your own personal relationship goals.

Think of it this way: if you were going to seek the ideal job, you would surely devote time and energy to putting together a resume. You would define your own professional qualifications and also be prepared to let potential employers know some of your strong points, such as: *you are someone who is reliable, flexible and can be there when needed; honest, humane and able to rise to any challenge.* Aside from the traditional methods of finding a job, you might ask many of your friends and business contacts if they know of such a position, or know anyone else who knows of such a position.

You might also put into writing the type of position you seek and the environment you'd like to work in. You might list, in a cover letter, the responsibilities you'd like to handle, how much you'd like to earn, the kind of benefits you'd expect, the kind of company for which you'd like to work for and where you want to be located.

If you'd go to such lengths in your business life, consider that, similarly, a search for the person who might become your partner in all of your life might be more effective if you know what you're looking for *before you start looking*.

The Romantic Resumé you've created after filling out the questionnaire will describe, in detail, who you are, who/what you are looking for, and what you have to offer to your potential mate. It will also identify what you desire, and expect, in a potential mate.

Love and Intimacy

It's important to define up front the kind of mate best suited to you, to clarify if you are ready and looking for a commitment, or just interested in shopping around, having fun and dating. As Mae West put it, "Men are my hobby; if I ever got married I'd have to give it up." Both women and men can use the Romantic resumé questionnaire to look toward the future, and also define the most appropriate people to date.

Past Relationships

Obviously, this process is designed to help you move forward. Keep in mind, it's not uncommon for people to initiate new relationships based on long-running relationship patterns, or to choose new loves based on the ones that came before them. The suggestion here, however, is to instead recognize what went awry in your romantic past, and utilize that insight to make new, more appropriate choices.

Since you are someone who obviously seeks to meet more men or women of quality, you might find that this process gives a whole new sense of direction to your love life. What came before can be used as a stepping stone to what's to come next.

Sari Locker, the host of Lifetime TV's *Late Date With Sari*, and the author of *Mindblowing Sex in the Real World*, stresses the importance of acknowledging both the good and bad parts of former relationships.

"Everyone learns about relationships from having relationships. The way I see it, when a relationship ends, you have to take the information you learn about yourself and how you relate to another person, and bring that into the next relationship. It makes the relationship better. It also makes the *choice* of the next boyfriend or girlfriend better."

A New Approach To Love

Sometimes it's appropriate to experiment with a variety of "types" of people as you search for a potential mate. It can help you further clarify goals, and you may find, over time, that what was important when you first filled out this questionnaire changes as you gain more insight through experience. Taking a business-like approach – *which is not the same as being business-like with the people you date!* – will give you a framework and an edge of emotional distance that may prevent you from getting too involved with inappropriate people.

Imagine this: Instead of making your dating experiences all about trying to impress people and getting them to like you, pretend you're an interviewer or a talent scout in search of the right person who will play a very important role in your life: The position of dream mate!

Don't Be Clueless

When you search for love without first defining what love looks like and feels like to *you*, you run the risk of falling into familiar dating pitfalls, feeling as if you've wasted your time again. You need more than a mental snapshot with less information than a fashion ad: *Clarity* is a key to connecting with the *right* Mr. or Ms. Right. Think back to all those times you were seduced by a person's packaging – their looks, charm, outward attitude and attention – only to find the partner-from-another-planet emerging as soon as the initial honeymoon period faded. Take what you've learned from all the successes you've previously experienced in romance, and build on that knowledge.

On Your Mark, Get Set, Go

Grab your pencil and be totally honest with yourself. This is for your eyes only. Assess what's really important to you, and think it through. This section will help you recognize which of your fantasies are meant to stay that way – *just* fantasies – and which are dreams that you really want to come true! The following is intended to gather information that will help you formulate your Romantic Resumé.

II

The Romantic Resumé Questionnaire

Let's Get Physical:

The first thing we notice about another person is how they look: From beautiful lips and chiseled chins to scuffed-up shoes and ill-fitted suits, it's normal to register what you find appealing or unappealing in another.

This is your opportunity to describe your fantasy man or woman – so go for it! It is totally acceptable – and appropriate – to clearly state your preferences in appearance, right down to eye color (this *could* be the co-parent of your future children). Then, once you've done that, make an honest assessment of just how important looks are to you. For instance, if you are very fit, it may be a turn-off to be with someone who is not interested in fitness, and that could be a block to becoming intimate. Then again, you might feel that if a person can achieve the intimacy you crave, then looks may not be so important. Describing what qualities are most appealing, and then prioritizing their importance, will help you assess what physical attributes are truly meaningful to you.

Keep in mind, this is about *your* personal preference – not what your best friend, or even this culture, thinks is attractive. It's also a chance to see how important it is for you to be with someone whose looks will be admired by others. Some women might feel Brad Pitt is the most attractive man on the planet, while others might prefer a Dustin Hoffman type. By the same token, while some men lust after *Baywatch* beauty Yasmine Bleeth, many men *really* may not care that much about traditional beauty. This section – and everything else in this questionnaire – is about familiarizing yourself with your own desires, wishes and preferences.

Describing Physical Attributes:
Some people have a preference for a specific "type" of person and others appreciate a variety of types. What's your personal type or types?

Example: girl/boy-next-door; rugged outdoorsy; artistic; fresh-faced; intellectual; looks like that movie star you admire, etc.

_____
_____
_____
_____

List some of the most important physical characteristics which, put together, add up to the look you love.

Example: blue eyes, long hair, thin/fit, under six feet tall, athletic, curvaceous, etc.)

_____
_____
_____
_____

Beyond "blond hair" or "looks great in a bathing suit", what else is important?

Example: a sparkle in the eyes, an honest face, gentle hands, soft skin, great smile, an air of intelligence, etc.

_____
_____
_____

What kind of physical presentation appeals to you – such as style, type of clothes and what the person projects?

Example: casual but elegant, looks great in Gap clothes, exudes sophistication and class, shy but sexy, etc.

_____
_____
_____
_____
_____

Now ask yourself: How important is each of the physical characteristics you listed? If someone has many of the personal qualities you dream of in a mate, yet does not physically fit the bill, do you think you could accept that? Keep in mind that if you are a person for whom looks are EXTREMELY important, it is better to accept that in yourself than to pretend otherwise, and maybe hurt someone in the long run!

Rate the importance of the following on a scale of 1 to 10

    Type _____
    Beautiful/handsome _____
    Build/figure _____
    Height/size _____
    Hair/eye color _____
    Style/wardrobe _____
    Turns heads _____
    Attractive to
    me personally _____
    Special requirements _____
    (i.e, cleft chin, dimples, long eye lashes)

Now, having identified the physical qualities of your fantasy man or woman, and rated their overall importance, write a succinct description of the physical look of your ideal mate. Be as specific as you can.

♥ *Laurie Sue provides the following example:* An Alex Baldwin type is my fantasy man, yet I'd also go for the unassuming good looks of an Adam Arkin type. It's important that he have a warm, embracing smile; and bright, expressive eyes, either ocean blue or very dark. A cleft on his chin would be heavenly! I'd prefer him to be between 5'10" and 6'1", and muscular, with great shoulders. Reasonably fit and trim would be good. He should have a positive attitude and an air of confidence. A man who can wear jeans, denim workshirts, sneakers, cowboy boots and a bomber jacket – and also look great in a suit – would set my heart afire!

Now you try:

_____
_____
_____
_____
_____
_____
_____
_____
_____
_____

Key Life Factors:

Key Life Factors are fundamental values, beliefs and practices that are at the core of all individuals; they relate to background, family and status in life.

We all want to believe that "love will find a way," yet past relationships have taught us that sometimes distinctions between people can cause divisions. Carefully rate and assess your needs in the following categories, because these are among the most static conditions you'll find in relationships. Asking someone to change these parts of themselves could be like asking someone to select a new birthday. Although it's always possible someone can make a dramatic life change – such as switching religions or giving up a comfortable job to start their own business – it's not realistic or fair to expect someone to alter their Key Life Factors for you. It's essential that you get as clear as possible about these values; it will automatically help tune your personal attraction "antennae" to the right channel.

Fill out one or more of the applicable statements in each category.

Age:
A. I'd prefer someone the same age, which is _____.
B. The perfect age range for me is _____.
C. Maturity, spirit and energy count more, but I absolutely wouldn't want to be with anyone younger than _____ or older than _____.

Religion:
A. I date only people of the same religious background, which is _____.

B. It would be nice to be with someone of similar religious and ethnic background, but I'm open to _____ as well.
C. Religious similarity is unimportant because _____.

Ethnic background and nationality:
A. It's important to be with someone of similar ethnic background and nationality, which is _____.
B. I think it would be interesting to be with someone from a different culture, as long as we have similar values and beliefs in the areas of _____, _____ and _____.
C: I'm open to meeting new people of any background and/or have a specific interest in the _____ culture.

Value system:
A. It's important to be with someone who shares the same values, because I feel strongly that _____.
B. I don't mind a match that is slightly diverse, but there are a few key areas that I insist on in a mate, such as _____.
C. I haven't thought too much about values, but it's probably a good idea if they agree with me on _____ and _____.
D. I couldn't be happy with anyone who believes _____ or does not agree with my ideas about _____.

Education:
A. I'd like the person to have an education at least commensurate with mine, which is _____.
B: I have a particular interest in people trained in the area of (medicine or law, for example) _____.
C: The person has to have at least graduated from _____.
D. Formal education is unimportant, as long as the person is __

The Romantic Resumé

Profession:
A. I need to be with someone in the same profession, which is _____, so they can understand my work.
B. I love dating people who are talented, creative and smart, because they inspire me to expand my mind and _____.
C. I've always dreamed of being loved by a _____.
D. I definitely do not want to go out with anyone who is a _____ or a _____.

Work Style:
A. I am very devoted to my work, and I'd like to be with someone who is passionate about what he/she does, and is as intense and dedicated as I am, otherwise _____.
B. Many of my social activities are geared around my work; I need a partner who is not as involved in a career, so that he/she can support me in my professional goals and _____.
C. I'd like to be with someone who finds work engaging and challenging; someone who is not consumed by work but who makes an effort to excel. Balance is most important to me because _____.
D. I don't really care that much about how the person feels about work or even what they do by day because I'm just interested in _____.

Income:
A I'd like to be with someone who makes the same amount of money as I do or at least _____.
B. It would be great to have a partner who is financially successful, has a lot of money and is generous enough to _____ and _____.
C. I am not really worried about what the other person makes, as long as _____.

D: I don't think I could feel comfortable with someone who has money issues such as _____.

Family:
A. I want a partner who values close family ties, and who is not adverse to becoming close to my family, so we can _____.
B. I want to be with someone who loves family, but keeps a mature distance from family politics, and does not ask me to attend family functions unless/until _____.
C. I could be with someone who comes from a dysfunctional or estranged family if he or she is emotionally healthy, or at least working on resolving any emotional issues that could be a block to intimacy or _____.
D. I have no interest in getting involved with a person's family life, because _____.

Now, based on what your have learned in the exercise, write a statement that communicates at least five most important life factors in a mate.

> ♥ *Again, here's Laurie Sue:* I've always dreamed of marrying a doctor, and definately have my heart set on a man who is a healer. Perhaps he will be a medical doctor, chiropractor, psychologist or social scientist. I would definitely consider a man in another profession, as long as he is intelligent, productive and passionate about his line of work. He should be loving, kind and giving; and a natural healer who has an interest in psychology as well as insights into the soul of a person. Whoever my life mate turns out to be, it is essential that we share spiritual values, core beliefs about life and love and the mutual intention to create a relationship unlike any either of us have

known. It's crucial that we share the same goals in childrearing. I'd prefer if he were American, Jewish and between 38 and 46 years old, yet if the right person comes to me in a slightly different package, I will greet him with open arms.

Now you try:

_____
_____
_____
_____
_____
_____
_____
_____
_____
_____
_____
_____

Living Habits:

Please rate the importance of these on a scale of 1-10:

| _____ non-smoker | _____ smoker | _____ doesn't mind me smoking |
| _____ non-drinker | _____ occasional | _____ likes to frequent bars |

____ drug-free	____ disease free	____ has similar health issues
____ health-conscious	____ vegetarian	____ shares same eating habits/diets
____ neat	____ reasonably domestic	____ able to tolerate essiness
____ shares chores	____ cleans up after self	____ cooks

Now write a statement that includes at least five of the living habits most important to you in a mate.

♥ *Laurie Sue writes:* I would like a partner who does not smoke or use drugs, and who drinks only on occasion. I want him to be in good health and take care of his health. I'd love to join him in healthy eating habits. It's important to me that he is neat and domestic enough to do his share of chores. I'd like him to really care about the home we share and contribute to it in the best way he can. If he's a good cook—that would really sweeten the brew!

Now you try:

_____
_____
_____
_____
_____

Compatibility and Commitment:

Aside from whether a potential mate is willing to wash the dishes or compromise and hire a maid, it's important to really be specific about the kind of lifestyle that would be compatible with your own.

First, answer some of these questions about yourself:

What are your hobbies and personal pleasures?

_____
_____
_____
_____

What is your typical schedule (night shift, day job?)

_____
_____
_____
_____

How much time do you see yourself spending with this person, either while dating or in a serious relationship?

_____
_____
_____
_____

Do you own or want to own a home, co-op or condo?

_____
_____
_____
_____

Would you be willing to sell your property or move?
_____
_____
_____
_____

Would you consider a long-distance relationship or marriage?
_____
_____
_____
_____

What are your favorite forms of entertainment and socializing?
_____
_____
_____
_____

Do you enjoy cultural events, theater, museums?
_____
_____
_____
_____

Do you enjoy, or desire, traveling? Where to?
_____
_____
_____
_____

If you're a homebody, how do you spend your time there?

_____
_____
_____

Do you want a committed relationship now or are you at least open to the possibility of a future commitment?

_____
_____
_____

How would you feel if someone you meet is not yet ready or available for commitment?

_____
_____
_____

Do you want to have children? What size family?

_____
_____
_____

Do you already have children, and/or would you want to be with someone who has children?

_____
_____
_____

How do you feel about pets? What kind in particular?

_____
_____
_____

Now, rate the importance of each of these qualities in a potential mate. Jot down any specifics in the margin. *(Example: "I want someone who shares the same hobbies and pleasures" or "I prefer someone who does their own thing so I can do mine.")*

Has hobbies and private pleasures	_____
Keeps similar hours/schedules	_____
Agrees on how often you're together	_____
Is a home/condo owner	_____
Both want to live in same place	_____
Enjoy similar entertainment and social life	_____
Culturally conscious	_____
Enjoys travel	_____
Is a homebody	_____
Wants/is open to commitment	_____
Is ready and available for commitment	_____
Wants children	_____
Already has children	_____
Has/wants pets	_____

Now, write a statement, based on the last two exercises, that highlights at least five essential needs and issues you have in the area of commitment and compatibility, and add an evaluation of the five top-rated commitment and

compatibility issues in a mate.

♥ *Once again, Laurie Sue:* I really love having new adventures, traveling and meeting new people – it's part of my hobby and an integral part of my lifestyle. I like to socialize, but I also enjoy staying home and watching rented movies and sharing private time. My schedule is very busy, so I'd like to be with someone who is also busy and very independent, but who can truly carve out a life with me. I'd like him to be based in New York and yet be mobile, and open to the possibility of also owning a place, together, in Montana, where we would spend time during the year. I want to be with someone who has his own interests and has built his own life, and who is also accepting and respectful of mine. It's important, though, that we build new dreams and carve out a life together.

Now you try:

_____
_____
_____
_____
_____
_____
_____
_____
_____
_____
_____

Integrity and Honesty:

Sometime we *assume* people are honest, or we don't give much thought to their integrity level. Rate the importance of these qualities in the first column. Rate yourself on these qualities in the second column.

	Mate	Me
Trustworthy	___	___
Reliable	___	___
Honest	___	___
Keeps his/her word	___	___
Calls as promised	___	___
Arrives on time	___	___
Respectful of your feelings and your time	___	___
Takes responsibility for his/her actions	___	___
Apologizes when appropriate	___	___
Acts maturely and reasonably	___	___
Responsive to communication and your needs	___	___
Works things through with you	___	___
Possesses self-awareness	___	___
Tells the truth about his/her intentions (for example, how open he or she is to marriage, or how determined never to marry)	___	___
Shares in the creation/ maintenance of the relationship	___	___
Admits when he or she is wrong	___	___
Well-regarded at work	___	___
Respected in community	___	___

Demonstrates in private all the
qualities he/she is known for
publicly as well   _____   _____

Write a statement about the five most important aspects of honesty and integrity in a mate, and another statement about the five areas in which you believe you excel.

Laurie Sue: I am an honest person who is respectful of others, takes responsibility for her actions, and acts with integrity and thoughtfulness. I am mature enough to communicate clearly and be responsive to another's needs. I want a partner with whom I can strengthen my ability to work things through in a relationship.

   I want to be with someone who is honest, has integrity in all he does and takes responsibility for his life and actions. I want him to be a good communicator who acts maturely and reasonably and is willing to share in the creation and maintenance of our relationship; this includes the ability to admit mistakes and to apologize when he's made one.

Now you try:

_____
_____
_____
_____
_____
_____

Personality:

We all have a sense of the kinds of qualities we are drawn to in another's personality. This is your chance to pinpoint the kind of person you would prefer to be loved by. This list will remind you of the wonderful and diverse qualities a human can possess – and how much you don't want to be around people with the opposite qualities. Circle only the ones that appeal to you most.

Funny   Sense of humor   Quick-witted   Prankster
Scholarly   Intelligent   Wise   Street smart   Naive/Innocent
Inquisitive   Interested   Interesting   Socially Aware
Romantic   Sentimental   Sincere   Poetic
Hot/Passionate   Sensual   Sexy   Not particularly sexual
Affectionate   Attentive   Generous   Appreciative
Cooperative   Disciplined   Freedom-loving   Balanced
Loving   Loyal   Independent   Dependent   Self-contained
Gentle and Kind   Flexible   Strong but silent   Steady
Compassionate   Caring   Empathetic   Helpful
Personable   Agreeable   Passive   Joyful
Open-minded   Inquisitive   Opinionated   Strong-minded
Driven   Ambitious   Aggressive   Assertive   Quick
Outgoing   Reserved   Conservative   Possessive   Coy
Charismatic   Persuasive   Seductive   Straightforward
Uninhibited   Courageous   Wild   Adventurous   Creative
Playful   Childlike   Cautious   Careful   Relaxed
Smooth   Slick   Sharp   Professional   Genuine
Serious   Intellectual   Respectful   Accepting
Spiritual   Intuitive   Positive   Exciting   Confident
Easy-going   Hard-to-get   Fun   Spontaneous   Casual
Great conversationalist   Good listener   Good storyteller
Mannerly   Courteous   Thoughtful   Instinctive   Expressive

Traditional   Unconventional   Non-conformist   Incorrigible
Forgiving   Humble   Unassuming   Modest   Happy   Spirited
Supportive   Available   Emotional   Sentimental   Sensitive
Energetic   Enthusiastic   Persistent   Homebody
Sweet   Soulful   Patient   Healthy   Magnetic   Aware

Next Steps

Now, go back over the qualities you circled, taking another look at those you did not circle, and assess which ones apply to you. Make a list of at least 10 of your most relevant qualities. Then make a list of at least 10 of the most important qualities you would look for in a mate.

> ♥ *Laurie Sue provides another example:* I am a compassionate, caring, loving, inquisitive, enthusiastic, open-minded, emotional, sensitive, supportive, sensual, adventurous, aware, slightly unconventional person with a great sense of humor.
>
> I'd like a mate who is: intelligent, spiritual, charming, outgoing, magnetic, sexy, personable, compassionate, loving, caring, wise, attentive, affectionate, self-disciplined, self-aware, flexible, open-minded, confident, great conversationalist, good listener. He's got to have a great sense of humor and be fun to be with!

Write down your own personality traits:

_____
_____
_____
_____
_____
_____

Write down the ten most important personality traits in a mate:

_____
_____
_____
_____

Now, consider some of these characteristics and rate the importance:

_____ Emotionally available and expressive
_____ Open to new ideas and ways of thinking
_____ Communicates effectively with partner and others
_____ Supportive and encouraging
_____ Can accept support and encouragement
_____ Takes a win-win attitude in relationships
_____ Is easy to talk to, be with and share ideas with
_____ Has a healthy attitude toward life
_____ Has a balanced attitude about men/women
_____ Is self-accepting and self-forgiving
_____ Accepting of diverse qualities in others
_____ Welcomes new challenges and opportunities
_____ Adapts well to change
_____ Possesses a good self image
_____ Is stable, steady and cooperative
_____ Is able to blend in with your family, friends, associates
_____ Stands out in a crowd
_____ Handles social, family and business situations well
_____ Is a maverick and non-conformist who does own thing
_____ Has qualities that match yours
_____ Has qualities that bring out and balance yours

The Romantic Resumé

_____ Fits into your life
_____ Inspires you to grow beyond where you are now

Now, go through each of those qualities again, and check off those that most apply to you. This is just a reality check to get a sense of the kinds of qualities that you will bring into a relationship.

Write down a statement based on this exercise that describes the *five* top qualities that you seek in a mate as well as a statement that includes at least *five* of your own top qualities.

> ♥ *Laurie Sue's example:* I am a woman with a healthy attitude toward life who welcomes new challenges and opportunities. I am very accepting of the diverse qualities in others; and, quite honestly, I am learning to be more accepting and forgiving of myself. I am very easy to talk with, be with and share with and I'm a great communicator!
>
> I am seeking a mate who is a great communicator in business, family and social situations as well as being a man who can communicate effectively with a romantic partner. He should be open-minded and fair, adventurous and courageous in his life choices, and emotionally available and willing to grow. A positive self-image is important. I would like to be with someone whose qualities bring out and balance my own. We can inspire one another to grow beyond where we are now!

Now you try:

_____
_____
_____
_____
_____
_____
_____
_____

Use the survey to assess your own relationship-readiness, and then begin to put those qualities in your Romantic Resumé. This is not a document that you will give out on blind dates, or in the first five minutes of meeting a new person. This is the document that establishes both your current state of mind and your relationship objectives. It is, in a sense, your "wish list". Keep it for your eyes only, or use it as a tool and a calling card as you network your way to endless romance.

III

How To Write Your Romantic Resumé

If you have already filled out your Romantic resumé Questionnaire, your Romantic Resumé has essentially been written! Remember all those brief descriptions you filled in? Well, they constitute some of the most important things you need to know about yourself and the kind of person you are seeking as a mate. All you have to do is put them all together—and they spell R-O-M-A-N-T-I-C R-E-S-U-M-'E. Laurie Sue, creator of the Romantic Resumé concept and all "examples," volunteers to be our sample Romantic Resumé.

Laurie Sue Brockway
c/o 847 A Second Avenue
P.O. Box 171
New York, New York 10017

♥

Birthdate:	December 18, 1956
Profession:	Journalist, author, speaker
Marital status:	Single, one child
Key Words that describe me:	Courageous, Adventurous, Inquisitive
Position to be filled:	Doctor of Romance/Partner In Life

Currently Seeking The Mate of My Dreams
An Alex Baldwin type is my fantasy man, yet I'd also go for the unassuming good looks of an Adam Arkin type. It's important that he have a warm, embracing smile; and bright, expressive

eyes, either ocean blue or very dark. A cleft on his chin would be heavenly! I'd prefer him to be between 5'10" and 6'1", and muscular, with great shoulders. Reasonably fit and trim would be good. And he should have a positive attitude and an air of confidence. A man who can wear jeans, denim workshirts, sneakers, cowboy boots and a bomber jacket – and also look great in a suit – would set my heart afire!

I've always dreamed of marrying a doctor, and definately have my heart set on a man who is a healer. Perhaps he will be a medical doctor, chiropractor, psychologist or a social scientist. I would definitely consider a man in another profession, as long as he is intelligent, productive and passionate about his line of work. He should be loving, kind and giving;, and a natural healer who has an interest in psychology, as well as insights into the soul of a person. Whoever my life mate turns out to be, it is essential that we share spiritual values, core beliefs about life and love and the mutual intention to create a relationship unlike any either of us has known. It's crucial that we share the same goals in childrearing. I'd prefer if he were American, Jewish and between 38 and 46 years old, yet if the right person comes to me in a slightly different package, I will greet him with open arms.

I would like a partner who does not smoke or use drugs, and who drinks only on occasion. I want him to be in good health and take care of his health. I'd love to join him in healthy eating habits. It's important to me that he is neat and domestic enough to do his share of chores. I'd like him to really care about the home we share and contribute to it in the best way he can. If he's a good cook – that would really sweeten the brew!

I really love having new adventures, traveling and meeting new people – it's part of my hobby and an integral part of my lifestyle. I like to socialize, but I also enjoy staying home and watching rented movies and sharing private time. My schedule is usually very busy, so I'd like to be with someone who is also busy and very independent, but who can truly carve out a life with me. I'd like him to be based in New York and yet be mobile, and open to the possibility of owning a place together, in Montana, or perhaps elsewhere, where we would spend time during the year. I want to be with someone who has his own interests, and has built his own life, and who is also accepting and respectful of mine. It's important, though, that we build new dreams together.

I am an honest person who is respectful of others, takes responsibility for her actions, and acts with integrity and thoughtfulness. I am mature enough to communicate clearly and to be responsive to another's needs. I want a partner with whom I can strengthen my ability to work things through in a relationship.

I want to be with someone who is honest, has integrity in all he does and takes responsibility for his life and actions. I want him to be a good communicator who acts maturely and reasonably and is willing to share in the creation and maintenance of our relationship; this includes the ability to admit mistakes and apologize when he's made one.

I am a compassionate, caring, loving, inquisitive, enthusiastic, open-minded, emotional, sensitive, supportive, sensual, adventurous, aware, slightly unconventional person with a great sense of humor.

I'd like a mate who is: intelligent, spiritual, charming, outgoing, magnetic, sexy, personable, compassionate, loving, caring, wise, attentive, affectionate, self-disciplined, self-aware, flexible, open-minded, confident, a great conversationalist and a good listener. He's got to have a great sense of humor and be fun to be with!

I am a woman with a healthy attitude toward life who welcomes new challenges and opportunities. I am very accepting of the diverse qualities in others; and I am learning to be more accepting and forgiving of myself. I am very easy to talk with, be with, and share with – and I'm a great communicator!

I am seeking a mate who is also a great communicator in business, family and social situations, as well as being a man who can communicate effectively with a romantic partner. He should be open-minded and fair, adventurous and courageous in his life choices, and emotionally available and willing to grow. A positive self-image is important. I would like to be with someone whose qualities bring out and balance my own. Together, we can inspire one another to grow beyond where we are now!

It Can't Hurt To Keep A Resumé Handy!

Of course, your Romantic Resumé doesn't ever have to go further than your desk, but it may be to your benefit to keep it handy for the use of others. Just as you never know when a job will open up, you never know when you might meet a fabulous new friend – or any other great contact – who can introduce you to quality people. The mere act of fashioning such a Resumé will actually bring your goals closer to reality – sometimes in seemingly magical ways.

You can create your Romantic Resumé by cutting and pasting your answers to the questionnaire, as Laurie Sue did, or fashion it any way you please. Here's another idea:

Step one: Carve out some quiet time to read over your questionnaire and then sit down and write a summary of who you are and what you are seeking. Use wit and charm, as long as you get your request across clearly. Sometimes we try to hide our agenda through humor and jokes. Remember, people respect others who are clear-minded and honest, and they will be inspired by your candor and resolve.

Step two: Use a business Resumé as a model, and include some of the staples: Name, phone number, birth date. And add in whatever else you would like someone to know up front: profession, whether you have any children, what town you live in, etc. Then sum up your relationship hopes and dreams in a couple of paragraphs. For example:

Joan Davis
Chicago, Illinois
(312) 000-0000

Born: 2/8/62
Employment: Account Executive
Family: Two children

Current Status: I am an attractive, smart, somewhat shy woman with a great sense of humor. I love traveling, photography and mushy movies, and it's important that I am able to express myself and my dreams to my partner. Although my work as an account executive keeps me very busy and "out there," I am really a homebody who loves cozy fires (I have a fireplace!), long, intimate conversations and dancing cheek-to-cheek in my living room. I am available for marriage but not anxious. I am very spiritual, and I play a mean game of chess.

Then continue, on the same page, creating your "wish list" of a romantic partner.

Currently Seeking: I am very interested in meeting a man employed in the world of business; someone who is smart and educated, yet different from the advertising and marketing types I meet daily. Although I would like him to be financially successful and stable, I don't expect him to pay my way in life. My children have a father who cares for them and helps support them, and I am just looking for a wonderful man to be there for me. Someone between the ages of 35 and 45 would be a good fit. It would be nice if he grew up with some of the same TV shows (The Brady Bunch) and music as I did, and has some of the same values. It's important that he be honest, open-minded and confident. And that he be a good talker, because I love to listen.

Dating Preferences: I'd like to hear first from any friend who knows someone like this guy, rather than receiving a phone call out of the blue – so please don't just give out my number. I am open to being introduced, or to brief initial meetings. I am new at this, so I'd appreciate your support in meeting someone using this method!

Good Journey, Networkers One and All!

Now, while it may seem weird to have a Romantic Resumé, remember, YOU DON'T EVER *HAVE* TO SHARE IT WITH ANYONE! It's for *you* – to get focused and climb toward the sky. You may find, with all the offers you get as a result of just putting this together, that it's easier to just hand over, mail or fax your Romantic Resumé.

At any rate, congratulations! You now know what you want – as well as having a sense of the romantic profile you yourself have to offer. Best of success to you as you begin the adventure!

PART TWO

♥

Everything You Need to Know About Networking Your Way to ENDLESS ROMANCE

This section is devoted to showing you a step-by-step approach to understanding and mastering the art of networking, and applying these businesslike techniques to meeting the mate of your dreams. You will learn what networking is, what it isn't, and how these skills will make your love life soar. You'll come away with the secret formula that will make your search for someone special a success!

Chapter 1

What Is Networking, Anyway?
...And How Will It Improve My Love Life?

First, for the sake of clarity, let's start with what networking *isn't*.

Maybe you can relate to this scenario: You walk into a "networking" event, pockets brimming with business cards, ready to shake hands with as many warm-bodied humans as possible. If you talk to a few of the suits milling about, you can tell the boss you worked overtime, making connections. And, if you're lucky, you may spot a handsome or beautiful potential prince or princess over by the buffet, who will turn out to be the person of your dreams.

You scan the crowd, eyes straining to read name tags, searching out all those people who have better jobs at bigger companies than yours – the ones who can *do something* for you. There are so many people that you're torn between making contacts that relate to your present job or seeking out leads for your next one. Underneath it all, you have this tiny little fantasy that you'll meet *someone* who is slightly more than a good business contact: a Saturday night date...an escort to take to your sister's wedding...a father for your child, perhaps. You've got that glazed, what-can-you-do-for-me look, and *you don't even know it*. When you finally do start talking to someone who could indeed be a very valuable contact, your eyes begin that scanning-the-crowd thing that eyes do when the person for whom they're doing the looking has ulterior motives. You have so many agendas for the future that you just can't stay in the moment.

It's not that you're a bad person or that your desires – to link up with the right business people, and perhaps find someone to date on the side – are inappropriate. In fact, when you think about it, it takes guts to walk into a room filled with strangers and make those strangers into new friends and acquaintances. It's just that the scene I've just described is NOT AT ALL what networking is about. Sure, you'll meet new people, and maybe even get dates, but if you don't bring genuine warmth and a certain openness to your interactions at such events, you will end up giving out, and collecting, a ton of business cards from people you barely remember, who will probably never call and whom you are not likely to date. More importantly, they won't *really* remember *you* either. I'd call that a no-win situation.

The term "networking" carries with it certain negative preconceived notions. If you've heard that networking is a matter of pouncing on people, handing out business cards, chatting up a storm (about yourself), saying clever things and ending with "Let's do lunch," then listen up, because *it's not like that at all*! I believe that, in its purest form, networking is an exchange of energy, a way of connecting with others. But you don't have to put up a front or put on a mask. It's simply a matter of being yourself – and, in the spirit of good communication, learning new ways to connect.

While the ultimate goal of this book is to give you a "training manual" that will lead you toward a more expansive and satisfying love life, it is hoped that along the way you will also have a great time. If you enjoy the journey of meeting many new people and of being yourself around more and more new people, then linking up with that special someone will become a natural and normal part of your life.

Isn't It *Un*romantic?

Some people feel that the concept of networking for romance

sounds very *unromantic*. I'd say it's *supposed* to: What we're proposing is a method that will unquestionably increase the odds that you'll marry your *"second"* husband or wife *first*; the intention is to provide a way to search for a mate with more precision. The process of networking for romance is not romantic, maybe, but the dating adventures that will *result* from taking this more systematic, business-like approach certainly are!

While I truly encourage you to try out *all* dating approaches that appeal to you, and utilize *any* method of meeting people, networking is no less romantic than a dating service or a personal ad – and it's safer, surer and *far* more productive than hanging out at a singles bar, hoping that the forces that be will lure someone perfect for you over to the general vicinity of your bar stool.

Like any new concept, networking for romance might take some getting used to. But remember, back in the seventies, the idea of a dating service was alarming to many single people, and the concept of placing or answering a personal ad seemed frightening. Back then, singles feared that they would appear desperate if they resorted to advertising, in any way, for a mate. These days, busy single men and women are desperate instead for better methods of meeting people – because they just don't have the time to hunt love down, or because they hate the hit-or-miss nature of random dating.

Anytime you put yourself out there in the dating arena, it's a risk, and that risk comes with the fact of being human. Yet I think you'll find that if you break down this challenge, pick it apart and see how it works, it's no longer so scary or foreign. Once you get over the learning curve with anything challenging, you are on your way to mastery. It becomes second nature.

Laurie Sue remembers a story she once covered that took her into an operating room to observe open-heart surgery. The surgeon talked to her the entire time he was doing a valve replacement, just as if they were sitting at a breakfast table.

"You literally have someone's heart in your hands," she said to him. "How can you talk and save a life at the same time?"

"This is what I do, every day," he said. "It is as natural to me as waking up in the morning and breathing." He knew how to take a cardiovascular system apart, and then put it back together again. He was aware of both the risks and the success rate of the surgery he was performing, he had a team of people supporting his efforts, and he was able to continuously monitor his patient for signs of trouble. He knew what he was doing because he'd trained for it, worked at it, and had enough experience with things going awry to know that sometimes, *those* things happen, too.

While medicine is not perfect, it is not all unknown. Some aspects are trial-and-error, and must first be tested in order to incorporate new ideas into the field. Well, dating is like that, too. The surgeon who now strolls confidently into open-heart surgery once had his own share of anxieties, too – cold sweats, adrenaline pumping wildly, momentary memory loss due to fear. Hey, that sounds like what happens to some of us on dates! But I'm here to tell you that you can learn to confidently network for matters of the heart, IF you are willing to try a new approach. So let's break down the concept and then put it back together again, with your *love* life in mind.

What Networking Means

Webster's Dictionary defines *network* as: *1. Any arrangement of fabric or parallel wires, threads, etc., crossed at regular intervals by others fastened to them so as to leave open space; netting; mesh.*

Let's substitute the word "people" in place of the words "fabric, parallel wires, and threads." With some additional minor adjustments, this is what we get:

Networking: Any arrangement of people crossed at regular intervals by other people, all of whom are cultivating mutually beneficial, give and take, win/win relationships with each other.

Of course, the word "network" carries many other meanings and connotations, particularly in the high-tech worlds of computers and television. Remember *Network* – the great movie with Faye Dunaway and Peter Finch? In the film, and in real life, "network" means a group of TV (or radio) stations under the aegis of a single, large umbrella company such as ABC, NBC, CBS or FOX. Well, the same principle applies to our definition of networking. In fact, it expands your mental picture of the possibilities for networking when you see that the *people* with whom you associate are interrelated in much the same way as TV and radio *stations* are interrelated through their affiliation with a major broadcast network. So bear with us while we give you the analogy...

The TV and radio stations belonging to a particular network derive certain benefits from such an association, like having access to their network's programming and news broadcasts. The network, in turn, derives the benefit of having its programming beamed into a particular city or "market," where the products advertised in its commercials have the potential of being sold. The more affiliates a network can claim, the more money it can charge the advertisers. This symbiotic relationship is a "mutually beneficial, give-and-take, win/win" situation for both parties.

The individual stations are able to tap into another benefit of network affiliation as well. I remember, years ago when I was a television news anchor for an ABC affiliate, that our station had the privilege of sharing local stories of possible national interest with every other local affiliate in the country. This mutual give-and-take was accomplished through what was called the Delayed

Electronic Feed, or DEF. Stations would contribute stories from their local communities through this system, and any other affiliate could choose to pick them up and use as its own. Imagine how much money was saved by each station, and how much more news was able to be shared with the viewing public. Truly a "win/win" networking situation once again, wouldn't you agree? And you'll see, as you read on, how the same basic concept can be made to work on a personal level as well – your own private network!

A Networking Graph To Help You Imagine The Possibilities

Here's a task for your imagination! The following mini-graph looks like a bunch of dots, yet it actually illustrates the basic set-up of your natural network – and shows how you are the center of your universe. You are also the very center of your own network. The dots represent the people who surround your life in so many ways, and the sheer number of those people begins to suggest how networking will lead you to endless dates and romance.

(Of course, everyone else is also at the center of *their* own universe and network – and that's precisely the way it should be.)

. . . .
. . . .
. . . .
. . . .
. . . .
. . . . YOU . . . .
. . . .
. . . .
. . . .
. . . .

Just think about it: Each person in *your* network can serve as a source of support (referrals, help, information, etc.) for you and everyone else in the network. And in turn, you and everyone else in your network can link up with vast numbers of people in one another's networks. Sound confusing? Hang in there with me, and realize this very important networking fact:

**WE ARE NOT DEPENDENT *ON* EACH OTHER,
NOR ARE WE INDEPENDENT *OF* EACH OTHER,
WE ARE ALL INTERDEPENDENT
WITH EACH OTHER**

The limitless, life-changing possibilities of this arrangement will really hit home when you realize that everyone in your network is also a part of other people's networks – people you don't personally know, which, indirectly, makes each of *those* people a part of *your* network, too. The sheer numbers involved here could fill this whole book with dots! When you begin to grasp the concept of linking networks of people with other networks of people, you'll begin to see how your dance card and dating calendar can very quickly fill up, as the dots in our little graph come to life!

Sphere of Influence

So where does this expansive, extensive, vast network of people come in? Back to you and the dots in the mini-graph: *Everyone* has a natural "Sphere of Influence." This simply refers to the people you know who are either directly, or even very indirectly, a part of your life.

Your sphere of influence includes everyone from immediate family members to distant relatives, and close friends to casual acquaintances. It also includes the person who delivers your mail, the plumber, the tailor, the person who cuts your hair, the neighborhood cop for whom you always have a hello, the people in the corner deli from whom you get your morning coffee, and many others.

In fact, your sphere of influence includes practically anybody who, in some way, touches your life, and whose life, in any way, you touch.

EACH OF US HAS A SPHERE OF INFLUENCE OF ABOUT 250 PEOPLE.

The best way to drive the point home is with a concept developed by super-networker Joe Girard, who, for fourteen years in a row, was officially listed in *The Guinness Book of World Records* as the world's most successful car salesperson. In his book *How to Sell Anything to Anybody*, he explains what he calls "Girard's Law of 250." The law states:

According to Girard, 250 is the number of people who will attend our wedding – and our funeral! He arrived at that number by asking a funeral director how many people normally register at a wake. Then he asked a caterer how many people usually attend a wedding reception. Both responses were "about 250."

Give or take a few, I'd say Girard is right on target! And I think we all have something to learn from this world-record holder, who built his business based on referrals, and worked his way to the top of his field out of a Chevrolet dealership in Detroit, Michigan. You may wondering, *What can a car salesman tell me about successful dating?* The important point to remember here is not necessarily Girard's profession, but what his "Law of 250" tells you about the huge possibilities for successful dating – just by tapping into your own network. And that's just the beginning.

To wrap your mind around the concept even further, you might want to take a moment to grab a pencil and paper and make a list of ALL THE PEOPLE YOU KNOW. I'd wager you can prove to yourself that the 250 figure still works out. If you have trouble thinking of every person you know or have known, jog your memory a bit by looking through your old phone books, photo albums, yearbooks and scrapbooks. Reminisce with your folks, your siblings, your best friend from college. You'll start to remember your great social studies professor, your first college crush, or that computer nerd who, for some of you folks, just might have been Bill Gates!

Enjoy yourself, too, as you recall the many people who have passed through your life: those that have stayed a while, and those who seemed to merely brush by, yet clearly touched your life as you touched theirs. Are you beginning to get the picture?

For more inspiration, or just for fun, look through the Yellow Pages under job classifications from A through Z, and ask yourself who you know in the various occupations listed. Or look at the names in the White Pages and ask yourself who you know with those same names. Who are your friends, co-workers, clients, customers, now? Who were they a couple of years ago? Who did you go to school with, or buy your car from? What about your television set? Someone must have sold it to you. What stores do you go to regularly, which ones infrequently? Do you say "hello" to the clerk? Everything and everyone counts.

Okay, I'll stop before I get carried away – I'm sure by now you get my point. Once you begin calling to mind your personal sphere of influence, you'll see that we all know a *lot* more people than we give ourselves credit for knowing. Count them up and you'll find the number will be right around 250. The dots in the mini-graph should be making more sense now, and as they begin to come alive, you might even find they have names and faces! Now let's take that a step further. Not only does everyone you already know have a sphere of influence of about 250 people, but realize this:

EVERY TIME YOU MEET SOMEONE NEW, YOUR CAN FIGURE THAT PERSON WILL ALSO HAVE ABOUT 250 PEOPLE IN THEIR SPHERE OF INFLUENCE, AS WELL!

Once a new individual becomes part of your network, another 250 people indirectly become part of your network as well. By cultivating friendships with new people, your own personal sphere of influence will *automatically* soar to incredible heights! Talk about connecting the dots! What with the people you know, the people known by the people you know, and the *new* people you are *about* to get to know, you might come to realize that you truly are a prosperous person, because you are tapping into a vast wealth of human treasures. You won't click with every single person in this great and growing network, but it certainly sets the stage for some astounding possibilities.

So What Precisely Does All This Mean?

You may still be wondering, *Exactly how will this dramatically increase my potential for meeting new dates and eventually, the mate of my dreams? And how will this have a positive effect on my life?*

The answer is: In a much different way than you might have imagined when you purchased this book. Let's break it down even further. First of all, when you went through the list of people you know (even if you just did it mentally), you probably came across a few former crushes that you thought of looking up again. And maybe you even remembered some friends of friends that you never got to pursue, even though they once made your heart beat like a big bass drum. You might even be thinking that Mr. Right could be that lawyer who handled your friend's personal injury suit, or that Ms. Perfect might be the charismatic real estate agent who sold your sister her home. You may even be thinking that *"The One"* is right in your own back yard!

But consider this: They are merely the tip of the iceberg – and before you start building a cozy little igloo with the lawyer or the real estate lady, remember that you might find romance on *any* of the little floes that chip off that ice berg! It's not that those two wouldn't be fine prospects, but when you realize the vast dating opportunities that await you when you follow this networking formula, you may find that you settled for someone close to home because you didn't imagine that your perfect mate was waiting for you just a few icebergs over.

Remember what was pointed out a bit earlier: Each of the people in your network is at the center of their own individual networks. Each of these people have the potential to connect you to at least 250 other people. And keep in mind, those 250 have their own 250. So now we're talking about 250 x 250 x 250. So far that's 15,625,000. And we only played out the 250 number three times! You do the math: With these vast numbers, the potential to meet some good people is so much in your favor.

Now, this is not to say that *everyone* in *every* network is a potential date. For example, we don't expect you to trot off with your best friend's brother, or start dating a co-worker's ex-wife, or for that matter anyone who is inappropriate. As I've said, the idea here is to set you up so you have access to a wider variety of quality people.

Here's how to whittle down the quantities: First of all, within those networks there is bound to be some overlap, people who know the same people. But keep going. Subtract the number of people who are of the gender that doesn't appeal to you. Now disqualify those who are already with someone, those who don't physically or emotionally appeal to you, and those who are not qualified prospects for any other reason in the world. You've weeded out a lot of people. BUT – you still have hundreds of prospects left!

You'll meet as many people as you could ever want to meet through the people in your natural network, plus those in the network you develop – if you apply the techniques included in this book.

This is where "Referral-Based Dating" comes into play. This means being introduced, by those in your network, to the kind of people you desire to date. Oh, and the deal is, you can date as many of them as you want.

Chapter 2

Referral-Based Dating: A New Trend in Romance

Turning "Blind Dates" Into "Referral-Based Dates"

Networking, as described in this book, is the road you take toward romance. What I call "Referral-Based Dating" is one of the most effective vehicles to finding the mate of your dreams. You may go on a few of these dates, or you may choose to go on many. But essentially these are dates with people whom you have met through other people in your network.

There are two ways to approach Referral-Based Dating: the *proactive* and *reactive* approaches. Each is practiced with romance – not business – in mind.

Proactive is more of a "call to action," in which you actively and strategically seek out people who can network you to the kinds of people you'd like to date. You may begin attending more social and business events, calling appropriate people to enlist their support and taking specific action almost everywhere you go. It's a way of utilizing your network to meet people you're interested in dating, *and* letting other people in your network know that you're looking for a special someone, that you'd be open to knowing any new people they might suggest.

Reactive is a more receptive, casual approach. It may take the form of telling a few networking friends that you're interested in dating, and asking them to keep you in mind if they should happen to come across someone appropriate. It may be a matter of just *making yourself* available to meet new people.

It's not as if you must choose *one* particular dating approach. In fact, the most effective way to network your way to endless romance is to utilize *both* the proactive and reactive approach. As you follow the program presented in this book, you'll learn how to weave in and out of both styles, according to what's appropriate for you at the moment.

For example, Melanie, a bright, attractive and self-aware woman, was benched from dating for a year after suffering a broken collarbone in a motorcycle accident. As she began to recover, she was anxious to resume a social life. She tried to connect with an old boyfriend (it didn't work), and went down the standard dating venues such as going to parties, scanning the crowds at social events and answering a few personal ads. When we met for lunch in New York one day, she was wearing that *I've-had-it-with-looking-for-Mr.-Right* expression on her face.

"At this point, I just want some companionship and fun," she said. "But I also would like to be with someone who is up-to-speed with me emotionally, spiritually and intellectually. Someone I *could* develop something with. So I'm putting the word out to all my friends and acquaintances – I want to meet some great new people. If they can just provide a link, I'll do the rest!"

She started slowly, mentioning to a few select friends that she was "looking," and casually asking them to keep her in mind (reactive approach); then, as she warmed up and gained confidence, she started a virtual campaign to meet someone special (proactive approach). She prepared a list of traits she was looking for in possible dates, and she enlisted some of the people in her network who she knew had access to quality people. Then she teamed up with a few girlfriends who were also single and looking, she let one of her health care practitioners set her up with some nice people, and became so open to being fixed up on dates that people thought of her all the time. They *wanted* her to meet someone wonderful! They *wanted* to help her make her dreams come true, and they knew that in doing so, the friends they set up on those Referral-Based Dates with Melanie would also benefit!

At last count, Melanie had met a number of terrific men in this way, and has become especially fond of one in particular. But as she says, "I never would have met this guy if I hadn't put the word out."

It's Fine To Start Out Slowly

Alan, a successful, good-looking guy, is not the type one usually thinks of as needing any help meeting women. When he returned to the U.S. after two years of working abroad as a computer programmer, he was too bewildered by culture shock to jump into dating; yet he was open to meeting a woman, if she happened to be *right for him*. "I told a buddy at work that after having been away so long, I'd like to meet a woman from my own culture, but I really wasn't looking for any serious involvement," says Alan. "I sort of wanted to get my feet wet. It's funny how things work: The very next day, after mentioning this to my friend, he comes into the office and tells me about a great woman who is an old friend of his sister. She had also been out of town for a while, and was in a similar situation. To top it off, she was a very attractive and warm person. We learned how to roller-blade together. Even though it never got serious, we helped one another readjust to being back home."

A "Blind Date" For The Nineties – And Beyond

Many people might consider Referral-Based Dating the same concept as the much-maligned institution known as "The Blind Date." I KNOW... you have plenty of blind-date horror tales to tell!

However, consider this: The idea behind Referral-Based Dating is that you proceed with wisdom and consideration for everyone involved. The intention is to communicate your dating goals so clearly, that the people you share them with get a strong sense of who you are and who you're looking for. It places the choice and the control firmly in your hands.

Although this may be reminiscent of a blind date, it's really not *blind* at all. Look at it this way: First, assume that the person setting up the date likes you. (If you have reason to suspect otherwise, then definitely *don't* accept the offer!) Doesn't it make sense that if somebody thinks enough of you to go out of their way to set you up with someone, they feel a personal interest in your well being? They probably know all about your likes and dislikes, the type of people you enjoy dating and something about the person they want to set you up with as well. If not, here's your chance to tell them: I suggest you fill out the Romantic Resumé Questionnaire *before* you begin the process, and be as clear as possible in your own mind, so you can then articulate the love of your dreams to those networking buddies who just may help you find him or her!

Doesn't it make sense that through Referral-Based Dating the odds are so much greater that you'll meet like-minded people, with whom you may develop a romantic relationship?

Proactively Meeting "Pat"

Let me give you another idea how to take the initiative in utilizing people in your network to meet others. For example, you want to meet Pat Smith (a fictional person). You search through your network for someone (or someone who knows someone) who can introduce you to Pat, or at least provide an opportunity for you and Pat to meet. Now, Pat might be the type of person who won't agree to meet someone without first knowing something about them. A referral from a friend in Pat's network, however, might make the difference. You might tell your contact that you spotted Pat Smith at a meeting, found her/him to be very attractive, personable and bright, and you're wondering if she/he is single. If it turns out Pat is free, you can take it a step further by finding out a little more about her/him, and sharing why you think it would be a good idea for you two to meet. In this way, by being *proactive*, you will be able to secure that initial introduction to Pat.

In the opposite vein, you could take a *reactive* approach: When you come across someone who happens to know Pat Smith you can casually say: "That Pat is really something...I'd love to meet Pat personally." That way, while your contact might not go out of the way to introduce you two, at least your interest is now known – and the introduction is probably not far behind!

A Referral-Based Double Date

Even those people who are initially resistant to the idea of Referral-Based Dating often come around when they realize how much they have to gain. In fact, a single person with many married or otherwise-coupled friends might find this a great new way to go on double dates.

Terri, for instance, is an attractive, recently divorced woman in her thirties, who had been in a funk, feeling lonely and *not* ready to begin dating again. One day, while visiting her lawyer, she met Linda, the attorney's office manager, and the two women struck up a friendship. Linda was also divorced, but had recently begun a long-distance relationship with Ron, a Canadian businessman.

It just so happened that Ron had a good buddy named Scott, also in his thirties and recently divorced. Scott, like Terri, was not looking to meet anyone. In fact, he had pretty much decided that he would live the rest of his life alone. It was easier that way, he rationalized. Scott was clearly putting up a defense against any potential pain by not looking for any potential dates – just like Terri. Having nothing better to do, Scott had flown to Florida with Ron a couple of times, when Ron visited Linda.

So, we have Scott and Terri, both lonely, miserable, and somewhat determined to stay that way. What they didn't realize was that in Ron and Linda, they each had a friend who loved and cared about them; friends who were determined to see them happy.

On one particular weekend when he was scheduled to visit Linda, Ron asked Scott to come along, this time to meet someone new. Meanwhile, Linda told Terri about a new guy she wanted her to meet. At first, both Scott and Terri flatly refused. After much convincing and, yes, pleading, they finally agreed to a double date – "But only informally, with nothing expected." "Of course," agreed Ron and Linda separately.

According to Terri, "The moment we met we knew there was a connection – something special between us. And what was so strange, was that the more we got to know each other in the months ahead, the more we found we had in common."

Terri, as of press time, is in the process of hurriedly selling her home in Florida so she can join her *fiancé*, Scott, in Canada!!

You may say that the Terri and Scott connection was just a fluke – a "magical connection" of falling in love at first sight. The difference in this case, however, is that *they weren't perfect strangers who met by chance*. Their friends, Linda and Ron, had carefully assessed the likes and dislikes of each, and made the decision to introduce them only after much discussion.

Because of their knowledge of the two people involved, Linda and Ron figured the chances were good that Scott and Terri would like each other. Whether they knew they'd be bringing two nice people together for a lifetime partnership, who can say; yet it was through networking that a beautiful relationship developed.

From this example, it's clear that blind dates need not be "blind" at all – *if* they are arranged by people in our network. Using the Referral-Based Dating system described in this book, you'll increase your odds even more for meeting a person high on your quality scale.

Matchmaker, Matchmaker...

If you're still not convinced that Referral-Based Dating is a viable alternative to random dating or downright loneliness, consider Lydia, a school teacher. Lydia thinks the proverbial "blind date" has a bad rep because many people believe that it implies they can't get a date any other way.

" *'Desperate'* is the word that comes to mind," she says. "I'd be afraid he would be a nerd, a person who would not be attractive to any other woman. A loser." Because of her ingrained belief, she refuses to even try Referral-Based Dating. Yet, she also confided, "I haven't had a date in six months. No...eight."

Although Lydia might someday meet the man of her dreams, right now she's lonely. And the only thing she knows for sure is that getting set up on a date is not her cup of tea. But intriguingly enough, some of the most romantic real-life love stories I've heard began with blind dates – including my own parent's! So, as you might think, I'm a big fan of bringing people together in this way!

Let me mention a few anecdotes just to demonstrate that "matchmaking" and "Referral-Based Dates" are as old as time. Think about it: Were the princes and princesses of pre-industrial

Europe allowed to carouse through the kingdom in search of dates? Did King Arthur meet Queen Guenevere at a singles' joust? Did your grandmother's generation sit home and *wait* for men to appear, or did they welcome the opportunity when a sister, cousin, aunt or friend fixed them up with good men?

"Mates have always been networked and pre-approved. It's been done that way throughout history," says celebrated science-fiction author Patricia Kennealy-Morrison – who also happens to be the widow of The Doors' Jim Morrison. As a rock critic and editor, she even met Jim through her network of business friends! In the years since her legendary husband's death, she's written many novels that contain details of authentic marriage rituals from the distant past.

"In tribal or medieval society, your connections would always set you up with someone suitable. Depending on your social status – men and women alike – your marriage would be arranged like an alliance, by your family, your tribe, your village, even the king. Marriage was a very serious business deal, and all factors were carefully considered. If romance in marriage happened too, that was a lucky extra; most people never had it and didn't expect it, though because the potential couple's compatibility was judged from the start by those doing the arranging, it came along more often than you might think. But whether you were a prince or a peasant girl, you almost never got to choose your mate for yourself. The ideal of marrying purely for love is a very, very recent development."

Of course, the Jewish tradition of matchmaking has always been based on the principle of bringing together a Jewish man and a Jewish woman for the purpose of "being fruitful and multiplying." (We're all familiar with Yenta the Matchmaker, of *Fiddler On The Roof* fame.) With Referral-Based Dating, you have the best of both worlds – a method of meeting quality people through other people you know, and, unlike the examples throughout history, *the choice* to pick the one who wins your heart!

"My friends and I have always networked naturally amongst ourselves, where romance is concerned," says Roberto Santiago, a New York City-based reporter and editor of the book *Boricuas: Influential Puerto Rican Writing.* "I have an opportunity to meet interesting people. And they all have interesting circles of friends. I think it can definitely be even more effective if you plan it out and follow this networking strategy."

How To Use Your Romantic Resumé

In addition to filling out the Romantic Resumé Questionnaire, you might also want to prepare your actual Romantic Resumé – as described in Part One. Obviously, it's not something you will be sending out on fax machines across America – although you certainly can make arrangements to fax it to specific people in your network. (Try to do this at a time when they will be there to receive it, or else it may get passed around the office water cooler clique!) The Romantic Resumé is more of an *as-needed* document that will save you from having to explain your romantic goals to every single person with whom you intend to network. It is especially handy to use for some of the group networking – for-romance projects detailed in Chapters 8 and 9.

When Laurie Sue was a medical reporter, a publicist friend of hers, Robin, asked her: "You know a lot of doctors. Can you introduce me to a nice MD?" When Laurie Sue mentioned Robin at her dentist's office, where she's friendly with the staff, the receptionist suggested that Robin write down her requirements and include a description of herself. Robin was so certain about her preferences that, instead, she put together a creative Romantic Resumé in the style of a press release. Robin ultimately did go out on a date with a doctor she met through Laurie Sue's contacts, but it turned out that simultaneously she began dating, and eventually falling in love with, a man in a different field. "At least I got to date a doctor," she said. "In a way, it was something I had to get out of my system."

The Romantic Resumé Questionnaire will help you clarify your goals, and the Romantic Resumé will aid you in achieving them – as well as help to re-clarify them as you go along. While the more qualifications you specify will narrow the *number* of people you meet, the better the odds will be that those you do meet will be your preferred type.

Keep Expanding Your Comfort Zone

Relationships are challenge enough these days. Why not at least make the process to *finding* someone special easier. The system outlined in this book is, as they say, "user-friendly." Just remember, along the way you may pass through some unfamiliar territory. It's important to recognize that it is human nature to: 1) take the path of least resistance; 2) avoid the unknown; and 3) maybe even to eschew new things before you try them, because you don't yet know what they *really* entail.

When it comes to matters of the heart, some people are struck by a paralyzing terror of putting themselves out there: a terror of being rejected or being looked upon as desperate. The question is: Will you let the dread of trying something new stand between you and fulfillment? Which would you rather cuddle up with at night: fear, or the mate of your dreams?

Trust me on this: Once you get the hang of it, the Referral-Based Date will be your preferred method of traveling to...*The Romance Zone.*

Chapter 3

Follow The Golden Rule To Endless Romance

Golden Opportunities Come To Great People

It's important that you lay down a foundation upon which to build – *before* you launch a personalized program to meet your lifetime mate. Anyone can utilize the techniques in this book and go off, pick up a phone and start networking. But without a strong and clear foundation it would be like handing out your Romantic Resumé to anyone who passes by and setting up dates with whomever will have you! It's an interesting idea, but will lead you back to the kind of random dating that has made you, on one or more occasions, wish you had a book like this to guide you on a different path.

In essence, your biggest selling point – in life and love – is who you are as a person. While success, money and external power certainly put a nice bow on any package, you might be surprised to find that the people who have all those things in life will be drawn to a person who has heart.

It may sound old-fashioned, but I can't stress this enough: Kindness, common decency and consideration of others go a long way in all aspects of life. And networking, in its simplest form, means being a kind, decent, considerate human being who is reaching out to others who share those same basic qualities. It doesn't mean being a saint or a martyr, but it does mean calling forth your best attributes and communication skills, and consistently acting in a manner that makes people feel as though they *want* to know, trust, help you...and assist you in lining up dates!

It's unfortunate that so many people learn early on in life to *manipulate, cajole and whine* to get what we want. Please understand that even though this book is offering techniques that will help you achieve your romantic dreams, they are being offered with the suggestion that you always try to *act from the heart*; that you incorporate these new skills and opportunities within the person you already are! You might find that, when you evaluate your own modus operandi for reaching out to others, you'll want to bring even more of your true self to each interaction.

New York relationship counselor and psychotherapist Barbara Glabman-Cohen often says, "All people are angels in human form." She believes that people wear masks to hide their true selves from others: masks of protection to shield against the deep feeling of vulnerability that always accompanies the search for love. "It's the mask that often drives people away, not the person underneath it," she says. "Some people believe it's the other way around!"

This is a good point to talk about how you will conduct yourself while carrying out your dating project: Would you rather express yourself naturally – therefore inviting people to express themselves more naturally around you – or would you rather wear *The Mask of Dating*? You know the mask I'm talking about – it's the one where you try to look good, say all the right things, do all the right things. The problem with *that* is that the mask can take over: Soon you begin to say things you wished you never had; you start getting nervous, you put up your defenses – and you defeat your own purpose.

Referral-Based Dating is simply a way to extend yourself even more, to reach out toward new opportunities to meet people. If you greet the entire process with an open mind and a smile, you, and all those you connect with, will have much more fun. Here are a few networking basics that will serve you well along the way.

The Golden Rule

Be someone who follows "The Golden Rule," and your life – and dating opportunities – will be golden as well.

There is a very valuable axiom when networking in the business world:

> **ALL THINGS BEING EQUAL,
> PEOPLE WILL DO BUSINESS WITH,
> AND REFER BUSINESS TO,
> THOSE PEOPLE THEY KNOW,
> LIKE AND TRUST.**

This is The Golden Rule – as well as bronze, silver and even platinum! – of business networking. For the purpose of networking your way to endless romance, replace a few phrases here and there: So The Golden Rule of socializing and dating should read like this:

> **ALL THINGS BEING EQUAL,
> PEOPLE WILL SOCIALIZE WITH,
> AND WANT TO HELP,
> THOSE PEOPLE THEY KNOW,
> LIKE AND TRUST.**

In the most basic sense, the intent of this entire book is to offer sure-fire techniques that will *position* you for your journey of getting to know people and letting them get to know you; and to create opportunities for them to like you and to trust you. It's up to you to show them, time and time again, what a truly great person you are. That's the basis for developing a powerful network. When you take that one step further into the realm of utilizing your network to meet potential dating partners, or life partners, you'll want people to be *motivated* to introduce you to those in their network that you want to, and deserve to, meet.

The ideal situation for anyone who is ready and willing to meet their mate is that everyone in your network *enables* you to do so; that they are confident enough in who you are as a person to shoot a few of Cupid's arrows on your behalf. You want them to be walking, talking goodwill ambassadors, delighted and enthusiastic about assisting you in your romantic search. If you're willing to follow the game plan outlined in this book, that won't be particularly difficult to accomplish.

You Are The Quarterback in the Dating Game

Once you've got your network sizzling with romantic possibilities, it's important to keep the whole process moving; it's your project, so you're the quarterback. The most important factor here is to stay in the game and not drop out because you're bored or haven't met the right person – yet. It's a mistake to believe you don't have to nurture and tend your network just because everyone knows you and likes you and trusts you. Whenever you reach any level of success at anything, you've got to act accordingly, and demonstrate that you aren't just a nice, positive and effective person *only when you want something*! If you are one of those people who jump into a project head first, and then lose steam and interest halfway through, think about creating some breakthroughs in your life by seeing this project through to the end – and showing yourself, as well as others, that you *do* take care of business, even when the business at hand is your love life!

So as you develop your external network, address the life-patterns that might impede your progress and ultimate success. *It's important to search within and assess: Am I willing to bring something of equal measure to the table?*

Things Aren't Necessarily Always Equal

No matter how well someone knows, likes and trusts you, you've got to continue to act in ways that justify their belief and confidence in you. If you tell twenty people you are anxious to meet their friends, and then act inappropriately if you go out with a few of them, word will get around – and your newly developed network will crumble faster than a stale cookie. No one wants to be out there "promoting" and advocating someone to their friends, only to discover that person may pose a risk to their reputation.

The following is a first-hand experience with all things not being equal. It has nothing to do with my love life, but it has relevance to what we're talking about here.

There's a local dry-cleaning company run by owners and employees who are nice people and who try to do a good job. However, it just doesn't seem to work out. For one thing, they don't listen to instructions (when you request *light* starch and your shirts practically walk to the door to greet you when you come in to pick them up, you begin to suspect there *may* be a problem). They also nearly ruined three of my favorite suits. On a personal level, I can genuinely say I know them, like them and trust them. Trust them, that is, to do practically anything in the world for me...*except* clean my suits. Obviously, the fact that they happen to be in the cleaning business doesn't work out too well for them!

After a while, despite my positive *personal* feelings about these people, I felt I could no longer justify either doing business with them directly or giving them my referrals. If they were anywhere close to being equal to their competition, they would continue to get my direct business, as well as my referral business; they're not, so they don't. Again, "all things being *equal*" is a key phrase when it comes to the business aspect of networking – and in the social arena as well.

Imagine, for instance, you have a friend that you would like to see involved in a healthy relationship, and you set him up on Referral-Based dates on several occasions. As far as you know, he's a great guy – when he's with you – but you get some feedback that he consistently acts out certain turn-off behaviors. Maybe he checks his messages a million times on his car phone while his dates are trying to talk to him, or makes sexual advances during the first half-hour of the date. Not a good sign. You can talk with your friend about making some adjustments in his personality, style or attitudes toward women, but is he open to feedback? Will he utilize it in order to improve his dating life, or will he forever act inappropriately?

If he's not interested in learning from any past dating *faux pas*, then every single time you reach out to someone on his behalf, you are setting up someone you know for a less than pleasant evening – *and* putting your own personal reputation on the line.

As much as you may personally like the guy, would you want to keep setting someone up who consistently makes you look bad? To my mind, that's akin to those nice, well-intentioned dry cleaners mentioned earlier. "All things being equal" is the key phrase for this aspect of networking. If any given situation is not a win/win for everyone involved, then don't get involved with it!

Let Your Network Pave The Way

On the other hand, once you start the process of networking your way to endless romance, you've got to master your own impulses to don the "mask of dating" at inopportune moments. It's natural to get a little nervous and start "selling" yourself to people who interest you, but *cut that out*! The whole point here is that you want the people in your network to do that *for* you, so that by the time you go out with a particular person, that person already *knows* how great you are.

Lisa, a journalist, recalls an experience a decade ago, long before she heard of Referral-Based Dating. She was at a social event, talking with a close male friend, when no fewer than three of his friends joined in the conversation. They were each handsome, personable, apparently successful and fun to talk to. "Surrounded by all these men, I felt like a Queen Bee in a pot of honey," explains the attractive and personable thirty-five-year-old. "And things got sticky when, instead of pulling my friend over and asking him to give me a hand, I began flirting and bragging about myself with all of them, at once. I was running on pure nervous energy and felt like I had to do *something* to get and keep their attention. But these men weren't getting to see the real me – they were seeing me in my let's-impress-men mode."

Now, this was not a good move because, although we all know that Lisa is a warm, wonderful and genuine person, these guys all thought she was, as they say, on-the-make. Lisa says she realized, in that particular situation, that blatant flirtation was a big turn-off. When she asked her buddy to find out if any of these guys were interested in her, he very gently explained that all three said "She's got great energy, but she tries too hard."

"My friend later told me that those men had wandered over to us because of me," says Lisa, "but rather than letting them gather around and find out who I was, I was practically performing for them. I could have been holding court and creating a moment of genuine intrigue and curiosity. At least one of them might have been interested enough in knowing more about me that he would have asked my friend to set something up. Instead, I was left holding the bag."

It could have been a devastating rejection; but Lisa turned it into a powerful lesson. "My friend suggested that next time someone he knows catches my eye, I ought to let *him* do all the work and champion me to his friends. If only I'd known about Referral-Based Dating in those days!" Obviously, Lisa's friend liked and trusted her enough to give her some tips, and was willing to help because Lisa was open to learning a little something from her awkward experience.

When you are open to feedback and willing to use it to grow, working at enhancing yourself along the way, people in your network will stand by you. Of course, if you keep blowing opportunities, they may not.

Does Who You Know Makes A Difference?
"It isn't what you know, it's who you know" – That's one of those clichés that can raise the hackles on some people. It may even conjure the image of a know-it-all business person, or an older uncle, who knowingly puts his arm around you as he smugly imparts this wisdom to you. Or it may make you feel like you're a user, a devious Catwoman who'll stop at nothing to get what and who she wants. If any of those stereotypical images are lodged anywhere in your brain, this is your opportunity to let 'em go!

Who you know is not only one of the truisms of real life – it's also one of the crucial realities of networking your way to endless romance. Consider this: You can be a deeper thinker than Einstein, more knowledgeable than a walking dictionary, but if you have no one to listen to your theories, or to validate your defining point of view, then your information, insights and brilliance aren't going to go very far.

Well, the same applies to dating and love: You could be the most wonderful person in the world. You could be the perfect catch for someone who just happens to be looking. You might be the person who could light up the life of your perfect mate! However, you have to be willing to utilize your network of people – those people *who you know* – to help link you to that special person!

Take it a step further and you will realize that in order to network your way to endless romance, it's not just who *you know*...it's who *they* know, as well! That's why it's important to make the people you know become aware of the kind of person you are seeking.

Look at it this way. You might know Jim, the manager of your local bank; you've even become friendly enough to chat every time you stop by to make a deposit. He may think you are a nice, respectable person, and he just might have a friend in the banking industry, or any business, who could turn out to be your special someone. But would he dare make the suggestion if you don't first make the effort to let him know you'd be interested?

Unless Jim knows that you're "in the market" to meet someone special, and unless he knows the type of person you're looking for, the thought of introducing you to that special person he knows might never even cross his mind.

Therefore, let's modify the maxim:

**IT ISN'T JUST WHAT YOU KNOW,
AND IT ISN'T JUST WHO YOU KNOW.
IT'S ACTUALLY WHO YOU KNOW,
WHO KNOWS YOU, LIKES YOU AND
TRUSTS YOU, AND KNOWS WHAT
YOU ARE LOOKING FOR***

I realize that's a mouthful, but there's more. That asterisk represents the most *important* piece of your romance project. It means: ***When that person comes across the one who just might be right for you.**

A Brief Review, Again, Of What Networking Isn't

I hate to hound you with this; but, again, before you jump into this project with the zest and enthusiasm it deserves, always remember: Although "networking" is one of the buzzwords of today's business world, and rolls off people's tongues with the frequency of "Let's do lunch," most people don't really grasp its true essence. It's crucial that you not only grasp it but that you make it yours: that you create the appropriate context for this idea within your own network of contacts.

Typically, people believe they are networking when they hand a business card to everyone they meet. The aggressive shoving of a card in a contact's face is often followed by "Give me a call – I'll cut you a deal," or, "If you ever need a whichamahoozee, I'm the one to call." That's not networking. That's just hard-selling, and it's actually the *antithesis* of effective networking.

Remember the story of Lisa, who tried so hard to "sell" her best qualities to a gaggle of men that she ended up turning all of them off? She learned first-hand that the type of people she wants to meet are not the type who find that sort of presentation appealing.

The point is this: Whether in building your business network or your social network, coming on too strong, talking incessantly about yourself and being "I-oriented", is *not* the way to success. Giving to others, supporting them in reaching their goals, listening to what they have to say – *those* are the keys to creating a win/win scenario for you and all those people with whom you network. That's following The Golden Rule – to a golden result.

Chapter 4

Networking Is For The Shy
Getting Used To Meeting New People

Anyone can network with anybody, practically any place and any time. This is a fact! Unfortunately, some people are so shy about meeting new people or going new places that they clam up just thinking about it, and disqualify themselves from attainting their goals before they ever begin. The techniques in this book will work for people who are *painfully shy*, just as they will for people who are *painfully talkative*! That's because they provide a structure, plan and reason to get out there – and techniques to use every step of the way.

You can learn to turn shyness into an advantage when you recognize that natural shyness, in and of itself, is a positive, appealing trait. That's because people who are on the shy side often have a welcoming presence, and they can be *great* listeners.

If you're nervous about these initial encounters, let me put your mind at ease by explaining that your greatest asset in meeting new people is already on your face: your smile. I'm sure you've heard the saying, "Smile and the world smiles with you." It can help you transform an ordinary situation into a joyous encounter, so remember that as you learn new ways to increase your comfort level in group situations.

You've Done This Before!
Everyone, at one time or another, is called upon to walk into a room filled with total strangers and somehow, some way, strike up a con-

versation with someone they don't know. In fact, that is an experience that occurs in most people's lives by the age of five – remember kindergarten? Unless you were one of those kids who couldn't wait to separate from your parents, get on a school bus and ride off into the unknown, you probably had a touch of separation anxiety. In fact, you might have screamed at the top of your lungs.

You were not alone. Many people still walk into a room the way they entered kindergarten: apprehensive, unsure, wishing and hoping that someone else will make the first move. As a kid, feeling like an outsider was probably the worst thing in your life. Any psychologist will tell you that this feeling doesn't necessarily fade with age, we simply build defenses to help ourselves feel more comfortable. And some people's defense is to fade away; to become, in a sense, invisible.

Rev. Sandra Lee Schubert, a counselor and interfaith minister in New York City, recalls how networking brought her out of her shell. She now performs marriage ceremonies, leads groups, and can walk into any room and make instantaneous contact; but that wasn't always the case. "My mother always used to say I was a late bloomer, and it was true," she says. "Social situations were difficult for me. I didn't know what to say, how to act. I felt out of the loop. I was always afraid if I opened my mouth I would make a fool of myself. It was safer to blend into the woodwork."

That began to change when she got involved with a variety of special interest groups. Although she found herself blending into the background, she observed what was happening around her, and especially noticed how *other* people networked. A talent for poetry led her to join a writing group, which in turn gave her the courage to read her work aloud and win acknowledgment. In the process, she discovered her own unique voice, and before long she was giving public readings to bigger crowds filled with interesting people. The confidence she gained in every group setting inspired her to push a little farther, and *make herself available* to even more people. She went from being a seeker to one being sought out by others.

You've probably heard the saying, "A journey of a thousand miles begins with the first step." Even though the concept is very practical, you will find that something almost magical occurs once you've taken that first step forward. Your grasp of *how it works* will propel you toward learning how to *work it*.

Networking doesn't require you to get up on a stage and perform, but you will find that it does bring you into more public arenas. Robert Siciliano, author of *The Safety Minute: How To Be Safe In The Streets, At Home, Abroad*, is a professional speaker. As an extension of his career, he got involved with acting and stand-up comedy: In his role as a safety expert, he's known as "The Lifesaver," and in stand-up, he's one of the Cannoli Brothers. He plays a similar role, as Carmine Cannoli, in the Boston-based interactive theater piece *Joey and Maria's Wedding*. The word "shy" simply wouldn't seem to apply to him – he's successful and seems very outgoing. Performing, he says, has helped him rise above shyness, and has boosted his communication skills in every part of his life.

"I'm shy in general and I'm shy with women," he says. "But when I have a role to play, it's like I'm really not responsible, so I can't fail. But I use the experience to build my emotional confidence and improve communication skills."

The point is: If attractive, personable and successful people have experienced shyness and still forge ahead in life, you can, too! You may not opt to be someone who speaks to groups, appears on television, or gets in front of a microphone, but you can find other ways to become more comfortable in unfamiliar situations.

Practice Everywhere You Go

One of the best ways to learn to meet new people is to practice meeting them everywhere you go. This includes weddings, PTA meetings, concerts, community events, political rallies, airports and any other locations where you find yourself surrounded by strangers. If life calls you into new arenas, why not consider them your opportunity to learn how easy and comfortable it can be to get to know others and be known by them.

You might try playing a game in which you challenge yourself to meet as many new people as possible at a particular place or event, and to learn as much about them as you can in a few minutes of conversation.

If you have never done this before, you might feel awkward at first: walking around, introducing yourself to strangers. But then, suddenly...the people around you are no *longer* strangers. You know them, their names, why they are there, and this process will forever demystify your fear of the unknown.

The whole point of this exercise is to relax and release the tension we all feel when surrounded by people we don't know. It can easily be applied to any situation, including those where the specific *intent* is to meet new people and develop a flourishing network. Again, to apply this exercise to your daily life, try striking up a conversation with just one new person next time you are at a public event. It can be a community festival, a school board meeting, a sale day at the sporting goods store...any place you happen to be.

The initial step can be to just say "Hello" to a new person. Next time out you can say, "Hello, how are you?" And the next time, ask a question or two about them, such as "What brings you here today?" Then try all three steps with another person. As you talk to more people, and get into lengthier conversations, you will gradually begin to increase your comfort level.

When you step up and greet the challenge of meeting new people, it eventually becomes less of a challenge and more of a way of life! Every time you approach a new person, you will be less uncomfortable. Soon, those first-time jitters – the nervousness you felt when you approached that first new person – will be far behind you.

Establish Ways To Make Yourself Feel At Home

Comfort develops from familiarity, and familiarity comes from practice. It just takes a little bit of extra courage to practice the unfamiliar. The fact is, networking is much more natural than most people imagine. You don't have to walk into a room and say, "Excuse me, but are you into a little networking?" You just *do* it, and the great thing is that the people you meet don't have to feel as if they are being "targeted" or that they are an "object" in your network.

There are other things you can do to increase your ease around new people; as you experiment, you will find that you will become bolder in your efforts to socialize.

Laurie Sue once struck up a conversation with a woman she noticed sitting near the wall at an event that was brimming with business people. The room was filled with good cheer and laughter; the woman seemed like a lovely, attractive person, and Laurie Sue was curious about why she was just sitting there. As it turned out, she was a very bright and articulate woman who worked as a librarian in southern California, and in her spare time was writing a book about consumer advocate Ralph Nader.

"I believe that people fall into two categories," she explained about her retreat from the activity. "There are those of us who like to be one of the first people in the room, so they can get themselves settled before everyone gets there and let the crowd form around them; and there are those who like to get there once the party is started, and mix in to an existing activity."

She went on to say that she is not of the latter group! As one of those people who prefers to get there first, she was thrown off-balance when she got there late. "I'm just trying to adjust myself to the rhythm here," she explained. "I'm one of those people who is more comfortable walking into an empty room and watching it fill up."

Although it may not always be possible to get to an event before the masses have arrive, it certainly makes sense to recognize your own crowd-comfort level, and make an attempt to proceed accordingly. Some people freeze up when they encounter a sea of unfamiliar faces, while others get an adrenaline rush. Think about planning your own encounters based on the category you fall into, and you will get a jump on increasing your comfort in any environment.

Learning To Be Assertive

Most people who know Laurie Sue would not consider her shy – at all! – yet she says that her comfort around new people comes from practicing over and over. Note the following:

> _Laurie Sue says:_ One of the reasons I became a reporter was because it gave me license to go out there and meet people – an excuse to go to events that would ordinarily trigger my shyness and prompt me to withdraw. As the youngest in my family, I grew up surrounded by the attention of doting adults. It was

truly a rude awakening to find that the world was not waiting to meet-and-greet me when I got older. I soon realized that it was up to me to create situations in which people would want to get to know me, like me and trust me. I had to learn to assert myself.

Meeting new people didn't come naturally to me, because no one ever thought to tell me *how to do it* when I was growing up. There was a time when I was terrified of unfamiliar groups, afraid that if I opened my mouth something dumb would pour out. The only way I could get past the fear was to keep putting one foot in front of the other, until walking toward my goals and dreams became natural.

Although "assertiveness training for women" is a concept from the seventies, there is a reason for its popularity: Women, more so than men, need to learn the "business-type" skills that will help them to conquer new environments. Men are more likely to be brought up with the notion: *OF COURSE they will walk into unfamiliar situations, take command of themselves, meet new people.*

It took a full-fledged Women's Movement just to introduce the idea that women didn't have to limit their accomplishments to the good work they do as "domestic engineers." It's only been a few decades since the major shake-up of those traditional notions, and women (more so than men) need more encouragement and assistance in being assertive.

This has absolutely nothing to do with male-bashing, or walking into a room like a bulldozer in an Ann Taylor suit. It's an inside job of giving yourself the "permission" to learn and utilize skills that will help you take control of your romantic destiny; and to devise an external support system that will help you achieve your goals.

As a reporter, I used my work to enhance my social skills, but it quickly became clear that I, like so many women, had to find a better way to make myself known in order to get what I wanted. When I stood up to ask my first question at a press conference, my knees shook and my lips quivered – but I did it anyway, and every time I did it after that, I would acknowledge my fears, and yet remember that I'd done it before, and that I would do it again. I used everything I could to get better at communicating and gain more confidence. That led to bigger – and emotionally more challenging – opportunities.

Along the way, I devised a game of "fake it until you make it." I identified my worst fears – meeting famous people, talking with certain kinds of business people, dealing with folks I perceived as authority figures – and conjured up a vision of how I wanted to conduct myself around them. For me, Lois Lane was a good role model: assertive, aggressive when she had to be, and *always* focused on her goal of getting a great story – or getting Superman. Those were two goals I totally related to! Lois never backed away from a challenge; she got into a million jams, but I could hear her chanting "Pulitzer Prize, Pulitzer Prize," to boost her confidence and quell her fears. Another goal I could relate to.

As I began to produce the Lois Lane vibe inside myself, while allowing my mind to brew visions of a successful outcome with whatever I did, I began to act accordingly. Although people knew I was "a fan," no one suspected that I was literally empowering myself with inspiration from a comic book character! Here's where the magic comes in: One of my favorite flashes of Lois Lane-inspired courage is the time I saw Christopher Reeve at a media event during the eighties.

Somehow, I got my mind to talk my feet into walking over and introducing myself. He didn't talk to me because I was a reporter, he talked to me because I went over and talked to *him*! I cherish that memory, because it proved to me that fantasy *can* become reality: I became Lois Lane for that instant and interviewed Superman!

My point is this: You don't need to have a press card or a reporter's pad – do you think I could take my eyes off his babyblues long enough to write down anything he said? You just need to be a little creative and daring in doing what it takes to reach your goals. I no longer needed to rely on external cues to trigger my confidence; it became a real part of who I am. I look at my Lois Lane period as my personal approach to assertiveness training. As noted psychologist, radio host, author and my good friend Dr. Judy Kuriansky observed at the time, I "used fantasy to imagine something into reality – and then actually had a fantasy come true!"

A few years later, I had the opportunity to meet up with Christopher Reeve again, and I thanked him for that moment and let him know it had literally changed the course of my life! He actually remembered our first meeting and seemed to genuinely get a kick out of all I had gleaned from it.

My story illustrates that the journey that leads you closer to your goal can be just as exciting as reaching that goal. "Role playing" can be an effective way to bring out that which already exists inside you – and it can make learning to network as much fun as actually mastering it.

Chapter 5

Looking For Love...
In All The Right Places!

One of the simplest rules of networking is to go where the kinds of people you want to know are likely to be. If you were interested in meeting someone in the teaching profession, you probably wouldn't find many great contacts at a meat packers' convention – even if you were able to wangle an invitation to the opening cocktail reception!

It's important to network in environments that are relevant to your quest for romance. Keep in mind, however, that the intention of going to a networking-accessible event is not necessarily to find your true love, but instead to put yourself in the sphere of influence of people who may be in his or her sphere of influence. If some of these suggestions seem premature, or make you apprehensive, take your time, pick and choose your options, utilizing every small success to build on the next.

Where Do I Start?

The list of places you can go to meet someone and initiate that first conversation is endless, and you've probably already tried a few. Remember also to look into organizations, groups and events that are *already* in your sphere. The following ideas are just to get you going.

To start off, consider some general public arenas. If you're in business for yourself, or work for a business, your local Chamber of Commerce is a good place to begin. They usually have several business/social functions every month, as well as committee meetings, educational seminars and sponsorship of many events. In Oklahoma City, for instance, the Chamber sponsors a chili bake-off that coincides with the State Fair and a huge rodeo. In Metropolis, Illinois, the hometown Chamber supports a host of activities during the annual Superman Celebration. In Brooklyn, New York, there is a very large business networking event called Brooklyn Works, which highlights the best of the borough. Hot Springs, Arkansas, boyhood home of Bill Clinton, has a vital Chamber of Commerce that sponsors everything from art shows to large celebrations. Once you begin investigating, you will probably find that your local Chamber has more social events on the calendar than you would have ever imagined.

If you don't want to pay the full membership fee to join your local Chamber, see about joining as an associate member. Typically, the fee is reasonable and well worth it. By belonging to such an organization, you'll have plenty of opportunities to set up some great, long-lasting relationships. Remember, as we talk about relationships in the context of networking, we don't necessarily mean romantic relationships; rather we mean relationships that are mutually beneficial, give and take, win/win relationships that could, through extended spheres of influence, lead to romance.

In the same vein, what about civic clubs and organizations? If you are someone who is interested in enhancing the community you live in (and everyone should be), then providing services for people who are unable to help themselves, or keeping the neighborhood crime-free by joining a citizen patrol, might be excellent opportunities to meet and network with like-minded individuals.

Women Supporting Women

How about women's organizations? There are literally thousands: Women in Construction, Women in Communications, American Women in Radio and Television, Women in Film, American Medical Women's Association, National Association of Female Executives, National Organization for Women – the list goes on. You can find local chapters of some of these organizations and many others in your regional telephone directory; or just peruse the White Pages under "associations" and related headings.

To a man, the benefits of joining a women's organization would be obvious! I know men who have done this and have met and dated many very nice women, and who have also met other nice women through their networking contacts. I would never encourage men to join *solely* to meet women; yet a man who joins forces with females with whom he shares professional interests might find it a very enlightening experience. He might also be appreciated, and noticed, for his contribution! In the spirit of networking as it's described in this book, it could be a win/win experience for all involved!

The possibilities for women supporting one another in romantic endeavors are endless, and women who are open to the concept will reap enormous benefits. Susan Crain Bakos, the author of several books, including *What Men Really Want* and *SEXATIONAL SECRETS: Things Your Mother Never Told You*, points out that through this method, "Women can easily support one another in finding love relationships in a non-competitive, non-threatening way."

A woman establishing the type of win/win networking relationships we're talking about, with other women in these groups, will have the opportunity to get to know great numbers of women who probably know great numbers of – men! You could hit a virtual gold mine of dating opportunities. I know many women who have done quite well utilizing their female networking contacts to meet potential dates – to everyone's benefit.

Join A Good Cause

Charities and special interest groups or organizations are also a great way to connect with like-minded men and women. For instance, if you are an animal lover, you can volunteer to work with your local Humane Society. Not only will you meet fellow animal lovers, but you'll meet people who know lots of other animal lovers in their network.

In every community across the country, you'll find an array of local groups focused on helping all sorts of good causes. Some are local chapters of huge national organizations, meaning that the romantic possibilities can be coast-to-coast. If you sign on to be a part of the solution to their challenges, you'll find that solutions to your own challenges (meeting the right people) will fall into place. In addition, you will find these relationships to be particularly strong, because people tend to bond over issues that touch their emotions.

The other thing about causes that tug on the heartstrings is that they attract so many socially conscious celebrities, which in turn attracts many socially conscious and giving volunteers and participants. Think Amnesty International (Sting, Bruce Springsteen), Farm Aid (Willie Nelson, Kris Kristofferson), Comic Relief (Whoopi Goldberg, Billy Crystal, Robin Williams). Can you imagine being a volunteer at some of these events? Smaller-scale opportunities will come your way regularly; they are opportunities to contribute while increasing your chances of meeting great people who are there for the same reason – to help out a good cause, and to meet *you*!

Laurie Sue recalls that in her early years as a journalist, she volunteered as production assistant on the annual Easter Seals Telethon, which at that time was held in her own hometown, New York City. It was a great cause to assist – and offered the thrill of working on live television. Contacts she established there were to prove particularly long-lasting: Even years later, when she'd come across someone who had also been involved in the Telethon but who had no clue who she was, she could instantly reconnect by saying, "Oh, we worked together on the Easter Seals Telethon." Because the event involved so many people, and was such a good cause, it continued to create instant rapport with people for years to come.

Fish Where The Fish Are Biting

This may sound obvious, but join groups or organizations that include the type of people that you want to meet. Position yourself near the front lines of that kind of person's profession, hobby, favorite sport. There's a saying, "If you want to marry a doctor, get a job in a hospital." More precisely worded, it might be: *If you want to marry a doctor, meet plenty of people who know doctors – attend a health or medical conference, and keep up with the latest developments in the health field.* Or give your Romantic Resumé to your family physician, your eye doctor, your chiropractor, your dentist, and tell them it would be good for your body, sight, spine and molars if you could fall in love with one of their colleagues, buddies or friends from medical school!

My friend, Rick Hill, an expert on business prospecting, wrote a book called *The Fishing Trip*. Rick's theory is "If you're going to go fishing, be sure to go where the fish hang out." Rick, who at one time was a record-setting sales manager at a radio station, would leave his office early every Friday afternoon to hang out at a local "fishing hole."

Rick wasn't goofing off – he was heading to the local club where advertising agency representatives congregated on Friday afternoons. Rick couldn't have put more prospects in front of him if he had issued invitations to a private party. And Rick's "fishing trip" technique also works when it comes to networking for romance. If you want to meet people of a certain type, profession, interest, etc., find out where they are and where they go, and then *go there yourself*! Another good piece of advice from Rick is to have numerous fishing holes lined up, in the event the fish just aren't biting at one of them. You might want to take just a moment to jot down some of your own prospective fishing holes, and alternative sites for your next fishing expedition.

Getting On The Right Track

If you're starting to pull your hair out just thinking of all the legwork – don't! This is supposed to be *fun*, folks, not an arduous task. It's like starting on a little branch in a big tree and using that branch to jump off to the next...and the next...and the next. Eventually, you'll get to the base of the tree, and then down into the roots – where you want to be.

You can find examples of good "tracking work" all over the media today. Watch any popular crime series (*NYPD Blue, Homicide*), and observe how detectives start with a supposition about how something might have happened, and then trace their way backward until they find out "who dunnit."

You can also take inspiration from movies that show you how reporters track down their stories. As Laurie Sue explains, reporters start with an assignment or premise; then they research everything they can find on the topic, call all their contacts who might have more information, assess the best way to get close to people they need to talk to, and start poking around for bits of information until they get the right leads. It can take an hour, or it may take months, depending on the who, what, when, why, where and how of it.

For a sense of how basic reporting skills might apply to your own quest – finding the right venues in which to make the best contacts – you might want to rent a few movies that feature reporters on a hunt. Films that may offer insights by illustrating methods reporters use in their work include *All The President's Men* (Robert Redford, Dustin Hoffman), *Perfect* (John Travolta), *Absence of Malice* (Sally Fields), *I Love Trouble* (Julia Roberts, Nick Nolte) and, Laurie Sue's favorite, *Superman: The Movie* (Christopher Reeve, Margot Kidder).

Once you get the sense of *where* you want to go, the *how* to get there will follow. I bet you'll find that once you open the door to new possibilities, the information you need will start showing up at every turn!

Breaking The Case – A Female Point Of View

In Laurie Sue's 20 years as a relationship reporter and through her work with PLAYGIRL, she has come across many trade secrets to share about getting into the general vicinity of the mate of your dreams.

> *Laurie Sue says:* I'm a firm believer in "where there's a will there's a way," and I know for a fact that you do not have to be *employed* as a reporter to employ the *skills* of a reporter.

Opening new doors may already be easy for you. The challenge is actually walking through them, and then seeking out more points of access – back doors, side doors, stage doors, trap doors, secret passageways and windows. In other words, you may have to poke around a little to find the right organizations, groups and events that will lead you to the right people. I have some tricks to share!

When I was Editor-in-chief of PLAYGIRL, I launched a feature called "How To Pick Up A...(You fill in the blank)." We'd select a profession or a fantasy man type and then set about exploring the best way to find them, meet them, hang out with them and date them. Many of the methods we used to go directly to the source can be utilized to get closer to *your* special someone!

Take cowboys, for example. We wanted to do a piece that told readers what these romantic legends are really like and where they hang out. As someone who believed cowboy boots were designed for fashionwear only, I wasn't exactly an expert on men who wear Wranglers, big hats and ride horses; but I was fascinated enough to want to learn more. So I went to a local western bar to get a sense of the cowboy culture. I bought a few books, clipped out related stories and called tourism bureaus in several cowboy states, asking for information by phone and in writing. I got my hands on some calendars of cowboy-type events all across the country, and called everyone I knew personally to ask which they thought was the best event for socializing with cowboys. The Annual Miles City Bucking Horse Sale in Miles City, Montana, was the winner – so that's where I went.

When I arrived, I was shocked – and impressed! – by the

endless sea of cowboy hats. By day, I watched rodeo, slipped backstage where they were getting ready to ride, and networked away with more cowboys than I'd ever hoped to meet. By night, I'd socialize with them at a big ol' street fair. I met rodeo riders, ranchers, horse owners, trainers, cowboy wannabes, drugstore cowboys and real cowboys. I was truly in the cowboy sphere of influence; it couldn't get much better. My mission was to do a story and tell readers how *they* can meet cowboys – not to link up with people who'd help me get hitched to a rodeo star! However, the process I went through and the result I created is exactly the kind of research, albeit on a regional level, that you yourself might want to engage in.

I also researched similar stories on doctors, rockers and men who wear tool belts. Obviously, your focus and requirements may be very different; yet it is not as hard as you might believe to get access to a place in which the kind of men you want to meet are milling about.

For example, there is an organization called The Young Presidents Organization (YPO) for corporate heads under 40 who run multi-million dollar businesses. They have meetings, social events, take cruises, offer courses and are involved in charities. If you are interested in someone of that ilk, you'd have to find out about local chapters and annual meetings, about upcoming activities that are open to the public, such as some of the charity events.

A local Chamber of Commerce, or Convention and Visitors bureaus has lists of conventions. You may see signs posted around your town or ads in the local newspaper. If you want to meet race car drivers, runners or golfers, and there's a race, a marathon, a golf game, get a ticket, and find out at the gate about any social events that will follow. If you love country music, go to Nashville, during the annual Fan Fare event in June, where you rub elbows with the stars and other country music lovers; or go anytime, because you can always meet great people there. If you want to meet authors and experts, go to book signings and events at bookstores, and attend workshops and courses at places like The Learning Annex in New York, California and Toronto. You will find the kind of people you are interested in sitting right in front of you.

You can access a myriad of information that will lead you straight to the sphere of influence that is home to the one who will become your true love. Good sources of information include: professional and social organizations, electronic media, newspapers, public courses and speaking engagements and, these days, the Internet.

Anyone can do it! You might have so much fun tracking down the venue that might lead you to Mr. Right that you may find yourself becoming even more open and able to *s-t-r-e-t-c-h*. Soon, you'll become an expert on your potential Mr. Right's hobbies and field of expertise. The entire adventure of finding him via creative researching techniques will bring your dream that much closer to becoming a reality. My advice to you is: *Go, girl!*

Chapter 6

Networking Step-by-Step
Winning Over the People You Want

Naturally, once you have done all the research we've outlined, you'll want to utilize the best ways to make contact with these new people – to get to know them, to allow them to get to know you, *and* to win them over.

Here is where the rubber meets the road: Unless you're willing to get out there and drive the vehicle you've designed, it's going to sit in the garage collecting dust with all the tools you've bought and never used. The easy, non-threatening techniques in this chapter will make it simple for you to increase your confidence and become more flexible.

Don't Shy Away Now
As we discussed in Chapter Four, people who are shy, or simply passive when it comes to meeting new people, might feel overwhelmed at having to go out and practice the art of networking. These techniques are designed with shy people in mind, as well as those who are highly extroverted and assertive.

As discussed, having "a role to play" in any given situation makes it easier to navigate through unfamiliar territory. Your role here is to network your way to endless romance! Be yourself; the techniques are designed to help you do what it takes to accomplish your aims!

Proceed slowly, and acknowledge that each step you take will build momentum and boost your confidence. These words, which echo constantly throughout this book, are worth emphasizing again: *Build upon your small successes.* They'll become large successes sooner than you think.

Picture The Following Situation

Imagine you have just arrived at an event – either strictly social or an after-work business/social event – and you don't know a soul in the room. Most of the people there are sitting at the bar, or hanging around the hors d'oeuvres table, either with people they already know or with someone they've just met. Many have drinks or something to eat, or are talking with someone. To the average person, this kind of socializing would constitute networking. Sharing some food, drink and conversation, however, does not a networker make!

You, having read this book, are ahead of the game, and can more easily establish the kind of relationships that will lead to mutually beneficial, give-and-take, win/win situations down the road.

While at this event, you might notice some people getting rather friendly, and perhaps even spot some infatuations-in-the-making. Remember, your specific intention is not to meet your dream mate over the buffet! It's not just these people you are interested in, but the individuals in their 250-person sphere of influence as well. The following strategies for success are networking principles. Although you'll be using them in a context of social networking, many are also appropriate for business interactions; since we are taking a businesslike approach to accomplishing your goal of building a social/romantic network, it is important to cover all your bases!

Networking Step Number 1:
Adjust your attitude.
By that, I mean you should remember that the overriding reason you're at the event is to accomplish a specific goal – the building of your social network. So approach it as work. You are on a mission!

That doesn't mean it can't be fun. Networking *is* fun! Establishing mutually beneficial relationships with people is fun. Having your dating calendar in overdrive is fun. Having social choices is fun. Since it's all new, it may take a while for the full impact of the fun factor to sink in.

If you still harbor any negative attitudes about networking based on bad experiences with what I call "wannabe" networkers, now is the time to ditch those thoughts. Networking is nothing more than creating open communication, a flow of energy and ideas between people in all areas of life. Networking techniques are just power tools to help you build dreams.

Networking Step Number 2:
Be open and approachable.
What I mean here is to be sincere, yet with an air of confidence. Be open, but don't try to cover any existing insecurities by coming off as pompous or arrogant. Be nice. Have a warm, friendly, but not over-exaggerated, smile on your face. Be aware of your body language: To people wanting to introduce themselves, do you appear open – or closed off? Maintain eye contact as much as possible, and try not to avert your eyes or "disappear" if you get a little nervous. If someone catches your eye, let them; don't be afraid to make contact in that way. Many people find it warm and inviting.

Laurie Sue noticed this effect when she was at a country-western dance club. She asked one of the cowboys why the women sitting up front were constantly being asked to dance, while she couldn't get so much as a twirl of the Texas two-step. "Because those gals keep saying yes!" he stated frankly. "A man knows he won't be rejected. It's obvious that they're open to dancing!" By maintaining an approachable attitude, these women ensured that they would be right on top of the action.

Project an aura of *Yes, I Am Here to Meet People, and Yes, I Would Like to Meet You*! It will magnetize people toward you. When you avert your eyes, turn away quickly, or have a serious or bored look on your face to mask your apprehension, it will be perceived as an invisible STOP sign.

Networking Step Number 3:
Introduce yourself to someone new.

If you need to warm up and get used to the environment, do one or more "practice" introductions. Be your sincere and charming self, and talk to *anyone* who looks friendly and approachable. It's a great way to get into the groove. If you are unfamiliar with the environment, it's a good way to get your bearings, and perhaps some information or insights on the crowd as well.

As you become more comfortable, introduce yourself to someone who is a "center of influence" type of person. These are the people who have a very large and influential sphere of friends, acquaintances and associates. They might be the most well-known persons in the room – a local dignitary, perhaps – or someone who is influential in the community, organization or company in which the event is taking place. Typically, these centers of influence have been a part of their community for a long time. People know them, like them and trust them. These centers of influence may or may not necessarily be successful in business, dating, or other areas of their life, but the point is, they know a lot of other people you might want to know.

But How Do We Find Them?
Obviously, you won't have difficulty spotting Tom Selleck or Heather Locklear in a crowd, or well-known business and community leaders, but what about the *unknown* centers of influence? You might think it will be tough, especially if you don't know anyone else at a particular event, but Rick Hill, the author of *The Fishing Trip*, has a great system for locating centers of influence.

He notes that, at most events, people are usually broken up into groups of four, five or six people. According to Rick, each group usually has a dominant, or most influential, person; a man or woman who seems to control or be the focal point of the conversation. Once you are aware of this fact, you will begin to notice how easy it is to find that dominant person in every group: When someone else in the group makes a point, all heads will turn to the dominant person for their response. When that person speaks, the others will hang onto their every word. You'll notice that the group laughs when he or she laughs, and agrees (or pretends to!) with whatever that person says. This is someone you want to get to know, because his or her opinion obviously carries weight with the crowd, and you can bet there are bigger, more extensive crowds in his or her sphere of influence. These are the people that magnetize others to them, and, down the line, they may be able to magnetize some introductions and dating opportunities your way.

Centers of influence may seem to create a bit of a whirlwind around themselves, and make things suddenly feel like they're hopping. Sometimes a lot of noise and laughter emanates from the area where they're holding court; just seek out the spots in the room where you feel the greatest concentration of electricity (the human kind), and there you'll find your center of influence.

You might also find the center of influence in a different arena. The person organizing or managing the event, for example, will know everyone. You won't find that person standing around and chatting, but you will find them – usually running around like crazy and handling a lot of logistics, problems and introductions! It could also be the opposite: The center of influence could be the person who is so confident about his or her ability to draw people that he or she gives each individual their complete attention for a certain amount of time and doesn't look up. You might have to wait, or to stop them on their way somewhere, to say "hello."

You might wonder how you can possibly get to know someone who already has plenty of people to hold their interest. First, don't assume that the dominant person is as charmed with that particular swarm of people as appearances may indicate; and remember, if there *are* so many people hanging around it's probably because this person is very open to meeting new people, and expanding his or her sphere of influence. You might have to be just a tad creative to grab the spotlight: As you're walking around the room, keep your eyes on the centers of influence. Eventually, one of them is going to leave their present group – to go to the rest room, the bar, the hors d'oeuvres table, or maybe just to meet someone different and new...such as you.

How You Introduce Yourself Is Important

Keep an eye on the proceedings, and as soon as the person you want to meet is breaking free from a crowd, make your move. You may have to very discreetly position yourself in the area so that you can monitor what's going on when the person starts moving.

Wait for your opportunity, position yourself nearby, and introduce yourself – that's perfectly acceptable behavior. If you're a bit embarrassed about introducing yourself cold, that's very understandable. Everyone has those feelings at times, including ultra-experienced networkers! But you must realize that if you approach someone politely and non-aggressively, that person will, 99 times out of 100, be quite receptive. A warm and polite approach will almost always get you the result you want; on some occasions you might find it useful to greet the person with a sense of familiarity – warmly, as if you already know or know of them. If they've touched you in any way, let them know it: "I loved your performance/your speech was so touching/I'm fascinated by your work – and I just *had* to meet you!"

After exchanging names, ask that person what line of business they are in; or, if you've had a chance to find out about them before you speak, pose a question related to something they are involved in or the event you are attending. This person will very likely then ask something about *you*. Keep your response brief, and then quickly move on to the next step.

Networking Step Number 4:
Focus the conversation to the most important topic in the entire world... THEM!

Everyone considers himself or herself the center of their universe. In fact, everyone *is* the center of their own universe. It's not narcissistic, it's simply human nature – even if he or she is a genuinely nice person. Much as it may seem almost *unnatural*, don't talk about yourself any more than you have to, and try not to launch into a neutral topic, like the weather, for an extended period. Keep the conversation centered on them. Though many of us don't like to admit it, and some people don't even realize it, the truth is, *we* are our own favorite and most important topic.

As far as I'm concerned, one of the absolute best books on this subject is the classic *How to Win Friends And Influence People*, by Dale Carnegie. Study this book and you will be amazed at how effective you can become at handling people. Much of Carnegie's advice is based on the premise that most everyone's favorite subject, cause, and concern is himself or herself!

One of the most powerful ways to win friends and influence people is to invest 99.9% of the conversation in asking others questions about themselves – and letting them answer, completely and fully! It doesn't have to be anything complex; you could include questions about their family, where they grew up, the schools they went to, their recreational interests or their business. Focus entirely on the person to whom you are speaking. This is known as being "you-oriented." Most people, of course, are "I-oriented," which is a no-no in this networking step.

Isn't it true that the people we find most interesting are the people who seem most interested in us? When you take this "you-oriented" approach in conversation, you are facilitating the "know you, like you, and trust you" feelings in that person; feelings that are necessary for a mutually beneficial, win/win relationship. This is almost always guaranteed to inspire the person you are talking with to think: *Wow. What a fascinating conversationalist that person is*! All you've done, of course, is ask questions and *listen*.

A publicist once told me the most significant thing he does to establish rapport is make the other person feel important. Using COSMOPOLITAN's legendary editor Helen Gurley Brown as an example, he said she is "extraordinary at making you feel that you are the most important person in the world – whether she speaks to you for five minutes or five hours." Laurie Sue points out that if you ever met Helen you'd know: She is the reigning queen of the "you-oriented" question.

The Open-Ended And Feel-Good Approach...

No one expects you to posses the interviewing skills of a professional journalist, but even Barbara Walters sits down to an interview with a few prepared questions. You, too, should prepare when you start your networking quest. Just remember, your intention here is not to elicit confessions – it's to keep the conversation flowing on a very positive beat. That's where open-ended, "feel-good" questions come in. You may already be familiar with the term "open-ended question." These are simply questions that cannot be answered with a plain "yes" or "no," but require a longer response.

I learned about the importance of open-ended questions as a television news anchor for an ABC affiliate in the Midwest. Station management decided there should be more live interviews during our nightly newscasts, and that the interviews should be about three minutes long.

Three minutes may not seem particularly long when you're scrambling an egg; on live TV, however, three minutes can be an eternity...especially with some of the guests I had the opportunity to interview.

Being interviewed under bright, hot TV lights is more difficult than it may appear from your living room – especially for the average guest, who is not used to being put on the spot while at the same time having to concentrate on sweating as little as possible. And though some of the guests who ventured to the studio for their three minutes of fame were solid and worthy people, frankly, they were a little lacking in the charisma department.

During the oil crisis of the early 1980s, I spoke to a local banker – let's call him Mr. Johnson – in a interview that made *me* sweat! The conversation went something like this:

Bob: So, Mr. Johnson, how do you feel the current oil problems will affect the local banks as well as the local residents?

Mr. Johnson: Uh...it's gonna be tough.

Bob: Okay...it's gonna be tough...can you elaborate on that, sir?

Mr. Johnson: It's going to be *really* tough.

At this point, I thought it would have been a fantastic time to take a commercial break, but no such luck. Through my earphones, I heard the director screaming, "No, no, stretch, stretch...you still have 2 minutes, 45 seconds left!"

Stretching an interview with someone who has nothing to say was torture, but it taught me that if I was going to survive three-minute live interviews with guests who didn't know how much they actually had to say, I needed to learn how to ask questions to draw them out – questions that would *get* them talking and *keep* them talking.

I had to learn a skill, so I went directly to the experts. I suggest you do the same, and tune in to some of the top network television interviewers – such as Ted Koppel, Larry King and Barbara Walters – and study their individual styles. Note the kind of questions that get guests to keep talking...and talking.

For networking purposes, stick with "feel-good" questions: these are questions that simply make the other person *feel good* about talking to you and feel good about you as a person – even though they hardly know you.

I have eight questions in my personal arsenal. They are not designed to be probing or busy-bodyish in any way; in fact, I have found them, time and time again, to be friendly and fun to answer. Remember, you'll never need to ask all of them during any one conversation – nor will you likely have the time – yet, just as a journalist goes on-camera with a clipboard of "in-case" questions, you'll be better prepared. You won't have to think so hard about the next question that the "interviewee" senses that you are fishing for something to say just to keep him or her engaged. As you get the hang of it, you'll find ways to adapt these questions to your own style and language, and the entire conversation will be much more spontaneous than it seems in print! Consider the person you are talking with, the situation, and the time-frame, and utilize them as needed. Tailor all questions specifically to the person you are engaging in conversation.

Open-Ended, Feel-Good Question 1: *How did you get your start in your business (line of work, or project)?*
I call this the movie-of-the-week question. Everyone likes to tell his or her story, don't they? Perhaps they are very proud of their own accomplishments and lifestyle, and would enjoy being asked to share them. Let them share it *with you,* and be prepared to listen – it could be a very long story!

I know from personal experience that this question is a sure thing. For example, shortly after a seminar I gave in Las Vegas, Nevada, I was sitting in a coffee shop having a bite to eat, when several people who had attended my seminar asked if they could join me. I welcomed them, and we began chatting. Then one of them innocently asked, "So, Bob, tell us – how did you get your start as a speaker?" Many (*many!*) minutes later, I caught myself still rambling on and telling my story. I responded to that question, too – and I was the one who had taught her how to ask it!

Open-Ended, Feel-Good Question 2: *What do you enjoy most about what you do (job, volunteer work, etc.)?*
Base your questions on whatever interests of theirs you already know about. This is a great question that elicits a good, positive feeling, and it will get you the positive response you're seeking. This is much more effective than the alternative, "So, what do you hate most about what you do...and, while we're on the subject, would you comment on your wretched excuse for a life? (Just kidding...but you get my point!) Stay away from anything negative.

Open-Ended, Feel-Good Question 3: *What do you do in your spare time (or for fun)?*
Again, you're getting them to talk about something positive, something they enjoy. It could turn out to be anything from a long, drawn-out discussion of someone's passion for stamp-collecting to an engaging conversation about a play they saw the night before. You may find you have some things in common at this point. Watch out for interjecting too much about yourself, which would be easy to do; keep focusing on the other person and make mental notes regarding what they say.

Open-Ended, Feel-Good Question 4: *What do you consider to be your major strengths?*
Obviously, this is not a question you can ask out of the blue. Ask *only* if appropriate, if it fits into the conversation thus far, and if it's used as a follow-up to something they've already said. There might be a smooth transition to this question from their answer to Question 3. If the person mentions proudly that they possess a black belt in Karate, or taught themselves to paint, you might be able to work it in.

I call this the "permission to brag" question. All our lives we're taught *not* to brag about ourselves and our accomplishments – especially to strangers – yet you've just given that person *carte blanche* to "toot their own horn." And, in all likelihood, since you asked, they'll do just that.

Open-Ended, Feel-Good Question 5: *What advice would you give someone just beginning in your line of work (favorite activity, sport, etc.)?*
I call this my "mentor question," and it's based on the fact that many people love to feel like a mentor or even a guru. It's a question that, in a very non-threatening, feel-good way, makes someone feel that their answer matters and that their advice is being sought. Give the person with whom you are networking a chance to feel important by asking the mentor question when appropriate.

Open-Ended, Feel-Good Question 6: *What one thing would you do, if you knew you could not fail?*
I borrow that question from famous minister, speaker and author, Dr. Robert Schuller, who asks, "What one thing would you do with your life if you knew you could not fail?" Everybody has a dream, and the person standing before you is no different. The question gives him or her a chance to share their dream, even fantasize about it, with someone who is actually volunteering to listen! They'll appreciate that you cared enough to ask, and often you'll find that they will take a few moments before they answer this thought-provoking, feel-good question.

Open-Ended, Feel-Good Question 7: *What's the strangest or funniest incident you've experienced in your business (hobby, sport, etc.)?*
This question provides the opportunity for this person to share a "war story" or two. Practically everyone has a great tale to tell about the "big one that got away," or an incident that was very strange, amusing, or maybe even a little embarrassing. Although they sweated through it at the moment, many of those events can become funny stories in hindsight. Sharing these stories can be cathartic for the other person, and it can make them feel good just to affirm that they survived it. Remember, most people – even those they love or have known for years – don't provide them with the opportunity, as you are doing, to share their heart.

Open-Ended, Feel-Good Question 8: *What one sentence would you like people to use when describing you and what you stand for?*
Laurie Sue says, for this question, she thinks of (who else?), Superman. What comes immediately to her mind is: "Truth, Justice and the American Way." Many people see themselves as someone who is known for something, and the mere fact that you're acknowledging it will be received as a compliment and a tribute. Almost always, the person will stop and think really hard before answering that question. Again, you are asking a question that perhaps no one – possibly even his or her own loved ones and friends – has thought to ask. The chances are good they've never before been asked that question by anyone – and they won't forget who asked it.

A Special Feel-Good Bonus: *"Tell me* **everything!"**
If you're the kind of person who brims with natural enthusiasm,

this can be used as a follow-up to an Open-Ended, Feel-Good Question – time permitting, of course! We borrowed it from our own wonderful publicist, Annie Jennings, and I've never seen it fail to elicit a response. Annie delivers it with such genuine warmth, interest and a sense of wanting to *hear it all*, that people are inspired to respond with a smile.

It's not a question for everyone. In fact, it's not even a question – but it is a good way to draw people out. If, with this, or any of the Feel-Good Questions, you sense the person's brain swimming because they don't know where to start, you can always toss in, "Oh, I know it's a big question...but I'm just so intrigued about you (your work, project, etc.)!"

It's Not Just What You Ask, But How You Ask

You may be concerned that a person will feel that you're being nosy, snoopy or just plain inappropriate by asking these questions during a first meeting, but experience has shown me time and again that the answer is "Not!"

Remember, you won't get to ask more than a few of these questions during your initial conversation anyway. But more importantly, these are questions people will enjoy answering. Of course, you don't want to come off like Mike Wallace of *60 Minutes* either, interrogating them or even just making them feel uncomfortable. Instead, these Feel-Good Questions are simply meant to establish an initial rapport.

Extender Questions

If the answers you're getting are still too short and sweet, don't fret – there are always Extender Questions. These questions are meant to *extend* the length of their answers, such as, "Really? Tell me more." If you just keep them in your consciousness as another way to keep a conversation flowing, the person you're talking to will have no idea that you got them out of this book! Usually, they'll be only too happy to keep on talking.

Then there is the "echo technique," taught to me by my friend and fellow speaker and author, Jeff Slutsky. According to Jeff, you only need to repeat the last few words of the other person's sentence to keep them talking. Watch the NBC comedy, *Seinfeld*, for a great example of this technique; Jerry and the other characters talk incessantly to each another in Extender-type Questions. Imagine this conversation happening between Jerry and his friend George, who, for our purposes, will be the "other person."

George (Other Person): "...and so we decided to go skiing."

Jerry: "Decided to go skiing?"

George: "Yeah, we thought that would definitely be the most enjoyable and cost effective event for most of the group."

Jerry: "For most of the group?"

George: "Yeah, you see, when taking into consideration the cost of..."

Of course, Jerry would probably wind up the conversation with an exasperated, "But George, you don't ski!" – but at least this gives you a sense of how Extender Questions work.

Jeff warns that we non-TV characters should occasionally adjust the wording of the repeated phrase, or eventually the other person is going to look at us and say, "What are you anyway – an echo?"

Another good conversational opener is the F.O.R.M method of asking questions. This acronym helps to focus our attention on what might be important to the other person by remembering that: *F* stands for (their) **f**amily; *O* stands for (their) **o**ccupation; *R* stands for (their) favorite types of **r**ecreation; nd *M* stands for (their) **m**essage, or what they deem important.

The One Key Question That Will Separate You From The Rest

There is one key question, appropriate for anyone you meet, that is an important step in the process of getting your new contact to feel as though they know you, like you, and trust you. It must be asked smoothly and sincerely, after an initial rapport has already been established:

"HOW CAN I KNOW IF SOMEBODY I'M TALKING TO WOULD BE A GOOD CONTACT FOR YOU?"

Asking this question is powerful because it separates you from practically everyone else in the universe. You might be the only person they have ever met who asked that question during an introductory conversation. It sets you apart, makes you instantly memorable.

During my business networking seminars, where I often address audiences numbering into the thousands, I ask for a show of hands from those who have ever been asked that question, or a similar one, by somebody they just met. Seldom do more than a few hands go up; more often, no hands are raised. It's very rare to hear that question from anyone.

But by asking that question, you are indicating to that person that you are concerned with their welfare and wish to contribute to their success and happiness. You are asking how *you* can help *them* – as opposed to the unproductive approach of trying to get them to do something for you, or to introduce you to someone before you've even left the event.

While some people may tell you that they can't think of anything that minute, you can be sure that they appreciate the fact that you even asked! Not to mention, plenty of people will come up with a response on the spot!

For example, if you're talking to someone named Val who sells copy machines, and you ask "How can I know if somebody I'm talking to would be a good contact for you?" Val might think for a moment and then say, "The next time you walk by a copying machine and notice that its accompanying waste basket is overflowing with tons of crumpled-up pieces of paper, that's a good sign the machine is not working well. The owner or office manager of that business would be an excellent contact for me."

The more people with whom you network, the stronger your networking power can be to help them produce results! You'll find that people really will appreciate your sincere interest, and, either then, or in the future, they will want to know how they can help you as well. Bank on it!

Asking this question will be the first indication to that person that you are somebody special and different, someone worthy of being a part of their social network. My advice is to learn that question word-for-word until it becomes second nature, until you could ask it in your *sleep*.

That one key question will serve your networking purposes throughout your life. No one will ever find it offensive that you have offered to help them in any way you can. Readers of my book *ENDLESS REFERRALS: Network Your Everyday Contacts Into Sales* tell me that this key question has been a turning point in their business relationships. And it will work in your social relationships as well: If you have even the slightest bit of hesitation about using that key question, practice it, and become familiar with it. You might fear that, in offering something to a virtual stranger, you are making it obvious that you want something back, but the truth is, people feel good when someone cares enough to do something for them. Don't offer anything you can't give, but share something you have with a new contact and many doors will open – for both of you.

Questions Are The Answer

Keep in mind that, whatever the situation, asking questions will generally keep things going in the right direction. Here's a story that confirms the power of "you-oriented" questioning:

Sydney Biddle Barrows gained notoriety after her book *The Mayflower Madam* hit the bestseller list. It was the true story of the rise and fall of the New York City escort service Sydney owned and operated as its madam. Sydney is a very elegant, attractive and proper-looking woman: Before her picture was plastered all over newspapers around the country, and on the jacket of her bestselling book, one could meet her and have no idea as to the line of work in which she was involved!

Understandably, due to the nature of her business, Sydney was not especially anxious for new acquaintances, and even some of her current friends, to know how she was making her living. Sydney's strategy for keeping her privacy was a very simple one: When someone asked her about her work, she would turn aside the question easily and politely by asking that person something about *themselves*. She kept her secret by using "you-oriented" questions – switching the topic of conversation to the other person, who was only too happy to respond.

Countless times, using you-oriented questioning, I've been able to establish excellent contacts on airplanes en route from one city to another. On one occasion, I kept a person talking about himself for the last 45 minutes of the flight.

As we landed I said, "If I can ever refer business your way I definitely will." He replied, "Me too," and I could tell he meant it. Then with an embarrassed smile he asked, "By the way, what do you do?" Amazing! Just by my focusing on him, he was totally sold on me before he learned any details about me!

Another time, I was sitting next to a syndicated columnist on a flight from Chicago to San Francisco. I wanted to talk all about my book, *Endless Referrals*, which was just about to be released, but I refrained. Instead, I asked all about her and her career as a journalist. The result was a feature story on me and my book that ran in newspapers all across the country – quite a nice boost when launching a new book!

Had I bombarded her with endless *fascinating* information about my book (fascinating to me but not necessarily to her) there's a good chance she would have closed right off and not been receptive. Instead, focusing on her first paved the way for her to like me, and only *then* for her to care about *my* project in addition. Investing your time in learning about the wants and needs of the other person is one of the greatest investments you can make.

You can always bone up on your ability to allow people to share themselves by turning it into a game: Challenge yourself to see how long you can keep someone talking about themselves. You don't need a reason, and that person doesn't necessarily have to be a prospect for your social network. Just do it to exercise your newly-discovered "you-oriented" questioning and conversational skills. Practice in supermarket lines, at the bank, with the waitperson who serves you coffee – just practice. You will find a whole new world awaits you when you master the art of asking "you-oriented" questions – and listening to the answers.

Back To Our Networking Steps...

Before you part company with new contacts, make sure you ask for *their* business card. Don't offer yours, just ask for theirs. Popular "centers of influence" are so deluged with cards that they sometimes get annoyed when someone hands them yet another unsolicited business card. If you are asked for your business card, and you happen to be a person who carries them, of course hand one over; but don't be insulted if the request never arises. Even though many people think a key to effective networking is giving out business cards, don't you believe it! (I'll explain more in Chapter 7).

Networking Step Number 5:
Before the event is over, deliberately cross paths with the centers of influence you previously met.

Let's say, toward the end of the event, you're standing at the hors d'oeuvres table by one of the centers of influence you met earlier. You can very pleasantly smile, and say: *Hi, Mr. Daniels or Hi, Tim. Are you enjoying yourself?*

That's guaranteed to make an impression, because, by this time, your new contact has more than likely forgotten your name! Again, nothing personal about it; you've forgotten people's names before, haven't you? By now this person has met a lot of people and heard a lot of new names. Most people are not good at remembering names. If you're one of them, keep that business card handy, and check it before you make your approach. At one time I was one of the worst at remembering names, but I decided to learn how to improve, in order to gain the networking edge I wanted. I promise you that after you call a person by name, he or she will take definite notice of *yours*.

Networking Step Number 6:
If you have the opportunity, introduce people you have met to each other, thus positioning *yourself* as a center of influence.

You can position yourself as a center of influence when you introduce people who can be of mutual benefit to one another either in their business or social life. By the end of any event, you will surely find that your networking skills have led you to meet one or more people; at some point, if you can bring them together to meet one another, it will make you the person who knows the movers and shakers.

I call this "creative positioning." Even though you're the one who walked in there in order to meet people who are centers of influence, you *yourself* are now one of those centers of influence, holding court. People will respond very favorably to your ability to bring them together, and they'll appreciate the fact that you thought highly enough of them to do so. That in itself will inspire your confidence, and thus bring you even closer to your goals.

Introduce each person by full name and mention what they do for a living, or their title; or, depending on circumstance, mention their favorite sport, a particular pastime, an interesting fact they take pride in. You can even mention something you might have learned from them.

For instance: "Mary Carter, of Very Big Rent-a-Car, I'd like you to meet John Billings, of Important Computer Industries. Mary, John was just telling me that he travels constantly and just had an irritating experience with his current rental company. John,

Mary may be just the person you need to talk to about linking with a more reliable service."

Maybe the people you meet the first time out won't be as specifically compatible – and maybe they will. It doesn't matter. Remember, something magical happens when the networking cycle starts up. Things begin to click and synergistic events begin to roll: You really do run into people like John and Mary, and can then introduce them to one another in a natural, casual way.

At some point during the conversation, excuse yourself, leaving the two you've just introduced to talk about the one common element in their life up to this point – you! You know they'll have only nice things to say about you because they feel you've gone out of your way to support them. When you touch base with them again, you can be sure they will know who you are.

Acknowledge Your Success

By the time the function has ended, you will probably have met about five or six good contacts. Even only one or two would not be a disappointing score – remember, a network of 1000 starts out with the first person (And, if you consider the sphere of influence factor of 250 people, you might only need four people in order to form that network of 1000!)

This is much more effective than just handing out business cards, or engaging in dozens of polite but relatively meaningless conversations with people you may well never see again. I'm not suggesting you act snobbish, or talk only to people who can be of immediate help; far from it!Be nice, polite and friendly to all, but focus more attention on the people with whom you're likely to have the most mutually beneficial networking relationship. Remember: You have a specific intention for being there, and it's not to chat with everyone. It's to build a network that will bring you closer to your dream. You deserve that dream!

You've taken a very personal approach, and it will pay off. You might wonder, If everybody knows these techniques, doesn't that take away the advantage? But look at it this way: These techniques are intended to result in a mutually beneficial, win/win situation for everyone involved in the process. The more people who know these techniques, the better for *everyone*.

In the next chapter, you'll learn the most effective follow-up methods for successful networking. They are simple in their application and they will add another personal touch to following up on all the new contacts you've made.

For another take on this, here's Laurie Sue again...

Communication Styles of Men and Women May Differ

Laurie Sue says: Now that you are totally prepared with feel-goods and extenders, and flexible enough to let communication flow in a natural back-and-forth current, I'd like to throw a possible curve: Men and women don't always speak the same language, and *women* may open doors relevant to your romantic quest faster than *men*. I believe it's just the nature of the species, and I'd like to offer these insights from my own female point of view.

Not every interaction or conversation is gender-specific, but if you heighten your awareness you will often find subtle (and not so subtle) gender-specific nuances. I believe a different dynamic occurs when men talk to each other, when a man talks to a woman, and when women talk amongst themselves.

Like it or not, everyone carries within them a vast cultural history, education and training specific to their gender and upbringing; it lurks in the subconscious mind and comes into play even when we are unaware. Because a multitude of other little nuances, experiences, beliefs and attitudes make every human a unique individual, it's impossible – and annoying – to make blanket generalizations. But there are certain things in life that I would separate out into categories of "guy things" and "girl things."

Perhaps comedian Rob Becker, star of the popular, one-man Broadway Show *Defending The Caveman*, sums it up best: "Men are hunters, women are gatherers." Thus, men are more likely to engage in conversations that are straightforward and designed to produce a result; communication with the specific goal of facilitating information or reaching a conclusion. Women, on the other hand, like to gab. Women like to "gather" information and share it. Men like to "hunt:" – make their point and move on.

Recognizing these basic – albeit generalized – instincts might just clear up a lot of communication challenges.

That Man-Woman Thing

It's been my life experience that conversations between men and women can be a whole other ballgame – not always, but much of the time. When men and women connect, any number of gender dynamics might kick in and therefore change the experience, and the result of the conversation. One dynamic, naturally, is sexual attraction. That doesn't mean the person you speak with will automatically desire you just because you are a woman; it just means the possibility of that kind of attraction may be present. Another dynamic may be that a man reacts to a woman in a fatherly fashion. A woman may resist that type of response, or she may totally enjoy and appreciate it. While women also take other women under their wing, or act as mentors, it's different when a man does it. I have been in so many situations that sizzled with male-female dynamics that I have come to learn that the best way to win someone over to your side is to let them be who they are.

For example, when I was just starting my career I was given a coveted crime beat. Although I was delighted by the challenge, I was petrified that the New York City cops I had to deal with would not take me seriously. There was a wonderful, older detective at the precinct house who sort of took me under his wing. He knew me, liked me and trusted me – and he knew I was a little green. At first, he paid *so* much attention to me that I found it overbearing and controlling. I was afraid if I let him help too much, I'd be indebted and therefore vulnerable. I feared he might someday want me to repay a favor by not reporting a certain item or toning down coverage. Truth is, he was just a good man who wanted to help out a young women he respected – me. Although it bothered me to think he wouldn't go out of his way as much if I were a guy, I had to admit to myself that I needed more help! It was the late seventies, an era in which cops were not accustomed to female *colleagues*, let alone female reporters.

He paid special attention to my journalistic requests, and he also let the cops in the precinct know I was, in a sense, under his protection. By doing this, he really helped me gain respect as a reporter (i.e., he cooperated with me as a reporter, and the other cops followed suit) and shielded me from any confusing sexual overtones, which were a given when you hung out around men in their locker rooms – which is where I often got my best scoops!

I came to really enjoy our flourishing friendship, and he, in turn, enjoyed the role he played in my life. It was a win/win for all involved: I got the information I needed for stories, the cops learned that I was an ally, not an adversary, and the people who read the newspaper I worked for were well-informed and safer in their community. If I hadn't put some effort into understanding his point of view, I probably would not have done as well on that somewhat overwhelming beat. I wouldn't have learned how to communicate with male cops in a language they would understand and respond to!

As Deborah Tannen, Ph.D., points out in *You Just Don't Understand: Women and Men in Conversation*: "If we recognize and understand the differences between us, we can take them into account, adjust to and learn from each other's styles...many frictions [between men and women] arise because girls and boys grow up in what are essentially different cultures, so talk between men and women is cross-cultural communication."

Some Insights on Women Connecting With Other Women

The environment you are in, and the people who happen to be standing around, may impact your approach to a person you want to meet, yet it is still possible to connect with other women on a very basic female level.

For example, women have the uncanny ability to reveal the most intimate details of their lives within a very brief amount of time, when given the opportunity – even while waiting in line for the ladies' room. Although following someone into a bathroom is obviously "stalking," running into someone you want to meet and starting up a conversation in the powder room is a wonderful – if weird! – way to make new friends. Hey, I've been in bathrooms with Demi Moore and dozens of other people I wanted to meet but couldn't quite get to in the main room of an event. It works, and it's a very natural, easy-going way to strike up a conversation. Great friendships have been born while women are freshening their makeup, straightening their skirts and resting their feet after hours in high heels! I would definitely include "powder-room talk" as a networking possibility. (Sorry guys: the door is closed to you, but you have your own men's room and locker-room activities, which women have for years been complaining they've been left out of!)

Another place to connect, with either gender, is the phone bank. I have done some of my best networking waiting for a phone to free up, or engaging in eye contact with people standing next to me. There is a way of saying *hello* with the eyes that can be followed up with a brief introduction – once the person has completed their phone call!

Chapter 7

Continue To Make An Impression
Follow-Up That Really Counts

Many of the new people you've met will walk away from that first encounter thinking you're a great person. However, this doesn't mean they'll immediately think: *Oh, he or she is terrific – I must introduce him or her to my friend so-and-so.* It *might* happen, but you want to get closer to it *definitely* happening. You've got to make them remember you, and inspire them to want to know you better. Follow-up is key.

Don't forget that when people are out doing business or socializing, they are almost high on the energy and enthusiasm of the gathering. They may even say "keep in touch" or "let's have lunch," and mean it in the moment – yet when they return home or to the office, they might forget all about you. Don't take it to heart – just take a personal approach to helping them remember what a great person you are.

What Exactly Does "Follow-up" Mean?
You probably already know that in business, follow-up means reconnecting with your contact soon after meeting, and pursuing new possibilities for working together or making a sale. Well, networking with the intention of ultimately finding romance requires a similar tack – and a particularly warm and friendly approach.

If you have the attitude, based on business experience, that follow-up is a royal pain, I encourage you to learn a new outlook: Follow-up can be fun and creative, and it can also be practiced in a systematic and consistent way that will make it second nature! That's what will separate you from the faceless others they met at the very same event. Remember:

NOURISH = FLOURISH

Follow-up is the first step to nourishing a new relationship for the purpose of helping it to flourish.

Do It Right Away
An important difference between those who succeed, in any area of life, and those who don't, is the ability to take action at the appropriate moment. The longer you wait to make that follow-up connection, the greater the odds are that you'll never do it at all. That's just human nature. Not to mention the fact that your window of opportunity is small, because that person will soon be off to the next event and the next crowd of new people. That's why it's crucial that you get into the habit of regular, immediate follow-up. Here are some suggestions to personalize your approach.

Send A Personal Note
Never underestimate the power of a personal note.

When you get your mail, do you automatically open the "junk" mail first, or do you sort through and look for the letters and cards with the most personal touch? They're the ones with a different shape, are handwritten, or look special because they are addressed to *you* as opposed to "resident." It's a good bet that the people you're following up on will remember a personal note, though they probably won't respond.

Your note shouldn't be a full formal letter – simply a handwritten acknowledgment that you enjoyed meeting them, or a thank-you for any words of wisdom or advice they imparted to you. It's both appropriate and impressive to express your appreciation, in writing, that they took the time to chat with you.

Writing thank-you notes is a staple of childhood, but don't confuse those notes your mom *made* you write – after attending a birthday party or receiving a gift – with your genuine desire to let a new contact know you are appreciative enough to follow up after an event. If you work in a sales-related field or public relations, where you constantly have to do follow-up if you want to stay in business, make sure that you separate the habit of "pitching an idea" or "making a sale" from just saying hello, and thanks.

When you send a note, you distinguish yourself from those who *don't,* which is almost everyone. I have found sending thank-you notes to be one of the most powerful tools in building a super-huge network, both professionally and personally. It's also been my observation that people with the most extensive business and social networks are avid note-writers. They utilize a system that doesn't take a lot of time and that can be done anywhere – on planes, late at night, when there's a lull at the office. When you show someone they matter to you, you will matter to them, and by making a simple effort to communicate you can gain their favor. It works the first time you follow up with them, and it will continue to work as you strive to nourish the growing relationship.

Notes Reaffirm A Positive Connection!

Laurie Sue once met a great guy at a conference, and they developed an instant rapport, automatically networking and sharing ideas. At the same time that she left the room to talk with someone else, he had to leave the conference to get on a plane. Although she figured he'd headed to the airport, she felt a little disappointed that there was no good-bye. Four days later, she received a note that said, "I had the best time hanging out with you. I wish I was able to say good-bye...all of sudden you were gone and I had to go catch a plane."

Even though she didn't take his abrupt departure personally, she *remembered* it. Sometimes a person's last memory becomes what they remember best about you, so it's important to keep those memories positive and friendly.

Notes can also turn a negative first impression into a positive friendship. For instance, at the annual convention of an association I belong to, I was sitting at a table with about ten other people where several conversations were taking place simultaneously. Without realizing it, I was talking more loudly than usual in an attempt to be heard over the noise.

I happened to be sitting next to a nice, older gentleman who is a true center of influence within the association; he and I had met just moments earlier. To my suprise, he turned to me with a touch of annoyance in his voice and said, "Bob, you seem to have quite an audience there." While he could have been a tad more tactful in his reproach, I got the message and lowered my voice. As soon as I returned home, I sent him a personal note – not an apology, but an acknowledgment – that read, "Thank you. It was a pleasure meeting you at the recent convention. Best of success in the coming year. Regards, Bob."

I didn't revisit the incident, I just let him know that it had been nice to meet him and wish him well. In this case, it effectively turned what could have been a negative first impression into a positive association. At the next convention a year later, he made his way over from across the room to shake hands and greet me, as if I were an old friend. He and I remain friendly to this day, and

I believe it is because of that personal note.

Joanna Poppink, a Los Angeles-based psychotherapist, points out that follow-up notes of any kinds are a way of cementing a fleeting possibility into a lasting relationship. "People I meet briefly, who, in the past would have only been pleasant moments, are now becoming more and more of a presence in my life because of these simple, appreciative notes."

Don't Delay

Write your notes as soon as possible after meeting someone. In many communities, you can mail a letter by midnight and have it on the person's desk, or in their home, by the next morning. Imagine how impressive that will be!

The basic follow-up note should be simple and brief, preferably handwritten in blue ink. Research indicates that blue ink is perceived as being more personal. It is also a color that stimulates a pleasant and relaxed response-think of blue ocean waters and blue skies. The tone of the note should reflect your own voice, yet still be appropriate for that particular recipient. For instance, if the person has a title and that's how they introduced themselves (such as "Dr.," "Mayor," "General"), address them that way. If you have any doubt about whether you are on a first-name basis, go with a formal "Mr." or "Ms."

Example:
Dear Ms. Sherman,

It was truly a pleasure meeting you at the Rotary Club. If I come across any opportunities that would be useful for you in your line of work, I will certainly send them your way.

John Smith

If you are on a more casual, first-name basis with your new contact, make sure you use a friendly, informal tone. For example:

Hi Dave,
Great meeting you at your company's hospitality tent during the Tennis Match. That was some game! Hope you enjoyed it too.
Best,
Janice Young

The Impression You've Made

Some people feel a little shy about sending notes to people they barely know. They might think: *I only talked to him for three minutes, he won't remember me.* Well, that's exactly the point! When you act immediately and make the effort to send a personal note, regardless of how you met, you have shown that you have manners and class – that you are a step above the average person they meet. You stand out as a considerate person worthy of being a part of their business and/or social network.

By the same token, you don't want your notes to ramble on with any strong sentiments or inappropriate comments, such as: "Gee, it's good to see the Rotary is finally inducting some female members." And you don't want to do too much storytelling, such as "I would have written sooner, but my dog got loose and I had to chase him and blah-blah-blah."

Less is more. Just say *Hello, nice to know you;* and get ready to create more opportunities for the future. You want them to get to know you, to like you and to trust you – and maybe *eventually* to hear more about your most important tale, that personal love story you want to create.

What To Write Your Note On

The more customized your note paper is, the more it – and you – will be remembered. Think about developing your own personal trademark, and having personal notecards, stationery or letterhead that represents your own special touch. People remember stationery and notes that are just a little bit different. You can design something that can be used for both business and personal communications, and that will accomplish the same effect – being remembered.

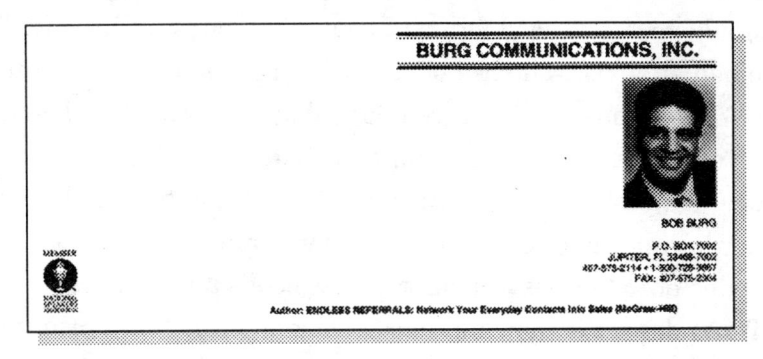

Actual size is 8 1/2 x 3 1/2 inches. Notice there is lots of space in which to write your note.

I use personalized postcards (heavier paper than the usual 20 lb. bond) that measure 8 by 3½ inches and fit perfectly into any #10 envelope. These can also be designed to fit in smaller envelopes. If you're in business, using personalized postcards is a natural. For example, you could put your company name and logo in the right-hand corner, and, beneath it, your picture; under that, include your name and contact information. Across the bottom you can run a one-line statement or motto relating to your business or the work you do, if you opt to make that part of the design.

Laura Norman, a leading foot reflexologist and author of *Feet First: A Guide To Foot Reflexology*, created clever notecards that said, "Put Your Feet In Our Hands," as well as smaller cards actually *shaped* like feet.

If you want to create something less businesslike, you can use the same type of format with your name and picture, and perhaps an inspiring or uplifting remark typeset across the bottom. Laurie Sue once received a beautiful personalized post card-type note card that read: "May the angels illuminate your path with love today." Imagine how many people were touched by that thoughtful expression.

Laurie Sue, who loves to experiment with catchy notecards, has had one customized for just about every phase of her life. She once had an artist render a photograph of her standing in front of the White House with a cellular phone in one hand and a reporter's pad in the other, and then had customized note cards made. Today she uses a caricature that illustrates her life as a busy working mom: She's sitting at her computer with her little boy piled onto her desk along with her books and articles.

These days, it's easy and inexpensive to design and print your card, whether you work with a professional designer, or do it yourself on your PC.

Every Picture Tells A Story

It used to be that only actors and models needed business calling cards, and such, with their pictures on them; but these days, everyone should consider it. Your picture is an instant, visual reminder of exactly who sent that note. On a typical day, people encounter a blur of faces; they don't always recall the face attached to a name, nor the name connected to a face. But they'll remember you, because *you* are giving them both!

They'll be thankful that it won't take any time or energy to remember you. The picture also stimulates an automatic *feel-good* response: They can visualize you and recall how you made them feel during your original conversation – a reaction that is now reinforced by the considerate note they've just received.

The should be appealing to the eye, the picture small, and leave more than enough space for the most important part – your message to them. If you're in business, please stay away from blatant advertising or tacky promotional gimmicks, such as "Jake's Restaurant: The Place Where People Love To Eat. Bring a friend and get a free glass of wine."

If you're one of those people who feels awkward including your photo, keep in mind that a small, classy picture, or even a fun caricature, will make people remember you and will enhance your networking effectiveness.

First-Class and Discreet, All The Way

As a general rule, you should put notes – even if they are postcards – in envelopes. Your contact will appreciate the extra personal touch – and also, possibly, your discretion. Who knows if she or he may be uncomfortable if you send a postcard that can be read by anyone? It may be, for whatever reason, that your contact doesn't want the world to know he or she attended the event where you met. Stay away from impersonal postage meters as well – your note may be mistaken for junk mail. Some of the most beautiful postage designs can be found right in your local post office, with stamps that feature historical figures, roses, sports and comic-strips. Be creative and always go first-class! If the person you are contacting is likely to be the recipient of huge piles of mail, try using envelopes with colorful designs and attractive motifs. Laurie Sue sugests, be sensible – don't send someone you met at a church function an envelope with big red lips or tiny hearts. But you can certainly tailor your envelopes to a particular person, or purchase a few dozen different kinds so they are available as needed.

In certain situations, consider overnight mail – when you want to touch base immediately with someone and be sure it gets there pronto.

Say It With A Greeting Card

If postcards, illustrations and caricatures are really not your speed, but you still want to do something distinctive, a greeting card is also a great way to send a follow-up note. With a card, the person knows that you went out of your way – or thinks you did.

If you are naturally a card-sender, this is a perfect vehicle for you. Go to a store and pick out a few cards you love, or a box of appealing notecards, and keep them handy; you can also find individual notecards and envelopes in some stationery supply stores. For instance, a woman named Rose can select any number of elegant cards with rose motifs. Or you can just select things that represent you in some way.

Lexie Potamkin, a close friend of Laurie Sue, is a public relations consultant and counselor who strives to be the world's most creative, warm and proficient note writer. Because she acknowledges *everyone* she meets in her travels, she always keeps a stack of personalized stationery, cards and stamps with her so she can communicate from anywhere in the world. Her trademark cards have been everything from flowers to formal monograms. If you met Lexie, you'd see that she radiates a beauty and charm that few people forget – in other words, she's as beautiful on the inside as she is on the outside. Her notes, cards and letters are also unforgettable, because they brim with appreciation and warmth.

"I believe that giving and receiving are the same thing," she says. "It feels good for both the giver and recipient because it is an exchange of energy." When you approach follow-up in this way, you can see it as a positive exchange between people. Nothing is expected in return, yet people will naturally want to do things for one another – because it feels good on both ends!

Keep Them In Your Thoughts

Now that you've made contact and followed up on your initial meeting, you'll want to make an effort to keep yourself in their thoughts. One of the things people appreciate most is valuable information, whether it relates to them personally or professionally. If you see a news item or come across information they can use, send it to them with another note.

My friend Ellen is an excellent model for initiating ongoing communication. She clips, cuts, faxes and mails things every time she encounters something relevant to a friend or contact. It's not a struggle or a job – she just does it because she loves sharing information. Sometimes she won't speak to someone for months, but when she does, she'll hear "Thank you for that article on such-and-such." Months later, they still remember receiving something of value – and thus, the person who sent it to them remains on their mind.

It doesn't have to be earth-shattering news. For instance, if you know that a person you recently met is working on a new invention and you then see an article about the U.S. Patent Office, you can send it along with a note: "Steve – Came across this and thought it would be useful for your project." Or, if you've met someone who loves antiques and you notice a new antique store that she may not know about, drop a line saying: "You may have seen this, but in case you haven't..." By extension, if you hear about a new class, or a new therapy, or catch something on TV, jot it down with as much specific information as possible, and mail it to the person. It's a nice, thoughtful thing to do, and one that will add to the positive association you've already begun to establish.

Remember, true networking is not a game of tit-for-tat, and if you have an *expectation* of getting something in return, people will feel manipulated. Even though you have a specific intention and a desired result, this technique is designed to build habits that become second nature-conduct that is assimilated into your daily life. When you do something for someone, without expecting anything in return, that person feels even better about having you as a part of their life. The founder of the National Speakers Association, Cavett Robert, said it best: "People don't care how much you know, until they know how much you care...about them."

Thanks For The Memories

The more effectively you can keep yourself on someone's mind, the better the chances are that they'll remember you when the time is right. When they are looking for someone to introduce to their great-looking cousin, or a terrific single co-worker, you'll be on their mind if you keep in contact!

Be creative and appropriate about mailing things to your networking contacts. Send little things, fun things, *not* expensive things-don't overwhelm them. A funny or cute card for a birthday, a holiday, or for no reason at all, a good joke that you recently heard, a calendar with your picture on it, a coffee mug, or any other novelty item-anything that can be useful or entertaining and that will bring you to mind often. Just don't overdo it!

Out Of Sight, Out Of Mind

I wouldn't be doing my job if I didn't share this example from my life. My friend Lisa and I often introduced each other to potential dates. There was a period of time in which we were in touch constantly, yet we lost contact for six months while I was on a speaking tour and she was busy with her work. When we finally spoke again, she updated me about a woman I had always admired from afar. This woman had been in a long-term relationship and unavailable for a long time, but had recently broken up with her boyfriend. Lisa had just set her up on a date with another guy.

I was a little shocked to hear that, because I knew that Lisa was aware of how attracted I was to this woman. When I asked her why she hadn't set her up with *me*, she apologized and admitted that since we hadn't been in touch for so long, *I just hadn't come to her mind*! My initial response was to groan, but it just goes to show you: Very rarely are we on someone else's mind as much as we would like to think we are. It's important to stay in touch!!

Thanks For The "Referral"

It's human nature to want to be appreciated for the things we do for others, so please bear in mind the following: When someone sets you up on a date with another nice person, *write them a thank you note!*

Be sure to follow up every dating opportunity that comes your way through a contact with a handwritten note. Something like, "Dear Mary, thank you so much for introducing me to Alex James. I look forward to meeting him and having a very enjoyable evening." It will simply reaffirm their belief that you were the right person to think of.

Make It A Habit

There's no need to feel overwhelmed, just take it step by step. It will soon become something you just do-like brushing your teeth. George Bush and Bill Clinton are both well-known note-writers; and, for better or worse, look where it got *them*!

It may be some extra work, but look at the whole picture: You're working on laying the foundation for a brand-new life.

Chapter 8

Putting Your Plan Into Action
Position Yourself For Referral-Based Dating

You've filled out your Romantic Resumé questionnaire, you understand what networking is all about, you've used the techniques to meet people; you've begun to develop a flourishing network that includes people you already know and many of the new people you've met. You're probably wondering *Now what?*

Now you are ready to utilize your network to help you enhance your love life. It's time to position yourself for Referral-Based Dating opportunities.

This will include telling people in your network that you are "looking"; and, as appropriate, sharing with them the Romantic Resume you have created. It may mean just describing the kind of people you want to date, or encompass creating special projects with particular groups of friends, fielding opportunities as they come your way.

If a little voice in your head is saying *I could never do that...I'll look too pushy or needy*, it's important to remember that your network now consists of people you have *already* won over. You are someone they know, like and trust. You have developed win-win relationships with these people and have shown them you are a caring human being. It will be only natural that they will want to extend the same to you. These are people who want you to succeed. But first they have to know:

1) *You are single and available*
2) *You are looking to "meet" others who are single and available*

3) The type(s) of people you want to date
4) That you are open to and interested in meeting people they know, know of or happen to meet

A "You-Oriented" Approach To *Your* Love Life

You've spent a good deal of time practicing "you-oriented" questions and, even though this is your time to make some "I-oriented" requests, the power of the "you-oriented" approach will continue to be effective. This chapter will give you some tips to get you started.

If the person to whom you're speaking is in a relationship, for instance, you might casually ask how they met their mate. They might enthusiastically launch into the uncut version of their own great romance story. As they do, any number of scenes will provide fodder for your next question, or you may just ask if *they* had a specific person in mind when love came their way. Since this will likely elicit some sort of response, you can always follow up with: "That sounds so romantic [or so exciting]. I would love to meet someone special."

Maybe this person will come up with some suggestions on the spot: a brother, co-worker, old friend who got divorced a year ago and is interested in meeting someone new. If not, the topic of romance has already been broached, and you can seize the moment to mention that you would appreciate it if they keep an eye out for someone who might be a good person for you to meet. When they ask, you can then tell them some of the qualities you are seeking in a date or mate. If you feel extremely comfortable with this person, you could even say: "You know, I am so devoted to finding someone that I've put together a Romantic Resumé. Would you mind if I send it to you?"

It's also possible to put the word out to your network in a more direct manner. This can happen by specifically contacting people to talk about it; and it can flow into an ongoing conversation on the phone, at work, over lunch or coffee...wherever. Here are just a few sample approaches...

To a single friend:
I think you're great! I'd bet you have a lot of neat friends. If you come across someone who might be appropriate for me, would you mind introducing us?

To a married friend who's obviously proud of the union:
You have an amazing marriage. I want to meet someone as terrific as your husband/wife. Do you happen to know any available terrific singles?

To an attached friend of the opposite sex:
I'm so lucky to have a friend like you... Are there any more like you out there?

To anyone:
I've decided to launch a full-fledged project to find my perfect mate and you are one of the first people I thought of to help me on my mission. (If the person is single add) Maybe we can support each other so that our love lives don't turn into "mission impossible."

If you feel even the tiniest bit reserved or embarrassed uttering these or any other statement that will get your point across (which is, remember, to "network" your way to endless romance), it is perfectly acceptable to start off any of the above statements with: *I feel a little awkward asking you (or saying) this, but...*

In time, and with practice, you'll not only get the hang of it, but you will invent creative ways to expand your opportunities and approach the topic.

Start At Your Comfort Level

Some people find it useful to throw themselves into it heart and soul, and practice *proactive* Referral-Based Dating. An analogy would be people who go on diets and, as a way of creating external support for their weight loss/fitness program, tell all their friends. They sometimes actively ask for support, such as going to the gym with a buddy.

Others take it slowly and proceed only when an opportunity presents itself, or by mentioning "if you should happen to come across anyone ..." That's the *reactive* approach.

Communicating romantic goals will vary from person to person. Your connection with some new contacts may be so casual and open that it's easy to share your romantic goals with them and enlist their support. Start with the people with whom you are most comfortable, and with whom you have the greatest natural rapport, and then work your way toward situations you consider more challenging.

It's important to recognize, also, that some of the people you now know are networkers by nature. Very naturally, without even thinking twice, they constantly connect people with other people. When you are ready to take it a step further, it may require nothing more than letting it be known you are open to and interested in meeting other single people and that you are ready to go on some dates. Then tell them, straight out, the kind of people you're interested in meeting.

They may *already* know someone who fits your description and, as you speak, they're considering introducing you. If not, chances are good that *you will be on their mind* when they eventually do come across the type of person you describe.

If the person you speak with happens to be single, ask what

type they are looking for. You might find that one of the best ways to seal a friendship, and at the same time accomplish your own goal, is to actually introduce them to that type of person as soon as you possibly can. That is a truly win/win approach to Referral-Based Dating.

Michael, for example, is a computer expert who was in the middle of a personal ads campaign to meet women when his business acquaintance, Louise, happened to mention she was also interested in meeting someone. They swapped information on one another's "types" and the kind of relationship they sought. Within a short time Louise introduced Michael to two friends, and though Michael did not have an immediate suggestion for Lois, he now constantly keeps her in mind when he meets new people – especially since one of her friends is someone he began to see regularly!

If the idea of "positioning" yourself for Referral-Based Dating seems somewhat contrived or premeditated...good! That means you are on the right track! You have carefully constructed your romantic networking project, and this is another level you're adding to the structure. I guarantee you that as the momentum of your romantic prospecting builds, so will your confidence and enthusiasm. Soon, you will learn to seize new opportunities as they occur, and before long the entire process will become quite natural.

Some Possible Scenarios

As you become more accustomed to the process of putting your plan into action you'll find opportunities in every day life. Here are just a few scenarios in which it you might find yourself.

The Coincidental Meeting: If you are spending time attending business and/or social events you will likely run into your new networking friends. Next time you find yourself standing by the buffet table, perhaps someone you *already know* through your networking efforts will happen by. You greet one another and chat. Regardless of whether you are both of the same gender, after a sufficient amount of small talk, you can *tactfully* bring up the topic of dating and finding the right person. Perhaps it is your response to the question: *So what have you been up to lately?* Bingo...an opportunity is standing right before you.

On-The-Spot Introductions: Perhaps, in a similar coincidental meeting, you are at an event when you happen to notice an attractive person laughing and enjoying a conversation with a circle of other people. You notice that person smile and wave to your friend. GREAT! The person you are standing with obviously knows the person you want to meet. You can say, right there and then: "Who is that?" After you assess from his or her response that this is not a person your networking buddy is romantically interested in (use common sense here, folks!), follow up with: "I can just tell from looking, from the way she [or he] laughs, that she is a fun person. Can you introduce us?" You are on your way!

Once you are introduced and begin to chat – using "you-oriented" questions, of course – and discover he or she is even more fun than you imagined, you can ask for a business card. If you know that the person is single, and sense that this person would like to hear from you, you may follow up on your own. If not, you can ask your networking friend to suggest you for a date.

The Party Possibility: Maybe you've been invited to a party at a friend of a friend's house. You arrive, meet up with the person who invited you and perhaps mingle with some of the other guests. You might spot someone who looks like the type you'd go out with in a heartbeat, but that person is engaged in conversation with a number of people she/he seems to know quite well. It would be awkward to just go up and say hi and maybe you're a little shy to begin with. You may ask your friend if she or he knows that person and discover that's not the case. However, the host of the party will know that person, or know someone who knows that person...and your friend obviously knows the host! Ask your friend to be your Good Will Ambassador and enlist the help of the host in introducing you to the person you want to meet.

Do It A New Way – Your Way

All the suggestions here are designed to get your mind percolating with ideas. Use common sense as you adapt them to your personal style and make necessary adjustments as you go along. Sometimes, the most difficult thing for anyone to do is to say, "Hey, maybe I'm the one who needs to stretch, to change a little, experiment more."

FOOD FOR THOUGHT:
Insanity is when we do the same thing day after day after day . . . and expect different results!

In other words, If you want the results these techniques can bring you, then either adjust them to you, or adjust yourself to them.

One of my friends and mentors, Bubba Pratt, says, "If you want to make some changes in your life, then you'll have to make some changes in your life." (Don't let the name "Bubba" fool you! This guy is a millionaire many times over. He's accomplished both his financial and personal goals by making a *lot* of changes in his life.)

So be brave and speak up about what you want – and who you want to meet.

Do Unto Others...

In business networking, the best way to *get* business and *get* referrals is to *give* business and *give* referrals. Anything you can do for the other person first (as long as it is done in the genuine spirit of giving) will come back to you many times over. Not always from that person, but somehow it will come back to you in a positive way.

The same holds true in the romantic arena, and if you look at life you will probably see many examples of times when you reached out to a friend or did something kind – just because you wanted to – and found that your own life seemed brighter and filled with more possibilities. Perhaps these had nothing to do with the people to whom you reached out to, but somehow, some way, the act of reaching out enhanced your life.

There are people who will disagree with that notion, and I genuinely feel sorry for them. They are often the same people who rarely go out of their way to help another unless there is an immediate payback – or at least a guaranteed return. If they are cynical and prone to believe "nothing works," they're right: Nothing works for *them* – because of their limiting belief system. Throughout your quest for the mate of your dreams, I encourage to be as open as you can to the many possibilities that come to those who set their dreams in motion and help others do the same along the way.

Chapter 9

Take Control Of Your Destiny!
No-Fail Methods For Meeting Lots And Lots Of Possibilities

People are always blaming their circumstances for what they are. I don't believe in circumstances. The people who get on in this world are the people who get up and look for the circumstances they want, and, if they can't find them, make them.
                                   – GEORGE BERNARD SHAW

There are many ways to actively and creatively work with people in your network to cultivate mutually beneficial circumstances in which all parties can make their dreams come true. When friends work together, they increase the power of any project by supporting one another in achieving the desired outcome.

Consider these typical examples: If you are in business, or involved with any groups with a common goal, you've seen the effectiveness of true teamwork. If you've ever planned a surprise party or even a wedding shower, you know the success truly lies in people working together to make it happen. If you've ever been in a Twelve-Step program, a weight loss or fitness group, reached out for support in approaching any challenge in life, or even attended camp as a child, you know the importance of the "buddy system."

An excellent way to position yourself for unlimited dating opportunities is to use some of the things you've learned in life's Basic Training 101, apply them to your goals, and stretch a bit to try out new ways of making things happen!

As long as your method for meeting people is legal, ethical, moral and safe, you can't go wrong with giving it a try. Just use common sense and your gut feelings to make clear in your own mind which joint projects are right for your particular needs. Look for the ways you can apply these ideas to your own unique circumstances.

The Buddy System

The world is filled with single people who want to meet other singles, and you can probably name at least one other person you know who shares your goal of wanting to meet and date new people.

Begin by calling that single friend in your network – of either gender – and proposing that you get together over lunch or a cup of coffee to discuss possibilities for supporting one another in your individual quests for romance. You might suggest that you swap information about single people you each know, and see if there are any "potentials" in either of your networks who would be appropriate to introduce to one another.

Naturally, you will extend this invitation to someone you know for a fact is looking. By now, you know enough about many of your new friends to know which ones would be open to the idea, and would feel the same way as you about this strategy.

Laurie Sue's friend Lillian says she has used this technique to accomplish many of her goals, and recently tried it out with a single friend who she knew was of a like mind. They met in a local coffee shop, discussed how they could support one another and then decided, since this would be an ongoing process, to develop a system in which to implement their mutual support. By the time the meeting was over, they had a plan!

First, they decided to swap a brief description or Romantic Resumé that highlighted what each of them was looking for in a man. Next, they put together a list of available single men they already knew. Then they whittled it down to the most appropriate people, agreeing to get in touch with them to check current availability and interest. By the time they left their one-hour meeting, they had arranged another meeting for two weeks later, and decided to talk on the phone in between. In time, the project became a natural process – and what seemed challenging at the start became second nature. While they did not come up with any prospects from their initial people-we-know lists, Lillian was able to set her friend up with a *friend* of someone from her initial list. Each of them continues to work on their joint project, and it's second nature to think of one another's goals when they cross paths with new people.

You might find that your friend is a little uncomfortable at first with the idea that you can communicate in such a way, but the benefits for you both will soon become obvious. Without being pushy or offensive, you can simply say, "Look, we're both nice people who are interested in meeting other nice people. Let's just go for it and have some fun supporting each other in getting to know more quality people." Don't be surprised if the person you ask suggests bringing yet another friend along. Perhaps he or she will immediately think of someone else who also is a nice person who knows lots of quality people.

Platonic Dates For Romantic Networking

Laurie Sue reports she has often tried the on-the-spot approach to meeting people with one of her closest male friends, Hank. They have accompanied one another to parties and events, as well as traveling together on vacations and business trips. They have known each other for so long that they've got their "routine" down to a science – but it all began when they met each other through networking, established rapport and agreed to support one another in meeting new people of the opposite sex.

Basically, it works like this: Whenever they go somewhere, they check people out to see if they spot anyone that the other would like to meet. Each keeps their eyes open for prospects for the other: If Laurie Sue, for instance, sees someone interesting across a room, Hank will make his way over, initiate a conversation and try to assess if the person is single, available, and as interesting as he appears to be from afar. If so, he will, in a tactful and enthusiastic way, tell that person about the wonderful, female friend who happens to be there. He'll either motion her over at the right time – after he's had a chance to tell this man about Laurie Sue – or he'll introduce her at another point. And Laurie Sue does the same for Hank.

They don't have to worry that people will think they are a couple, because they actively approach people rather than just waiting to be approached; and then they communicate on each other's behalf, making it clear that their own relationship is a platonic one. On many occasions they have spotted terrific people for each other, and have taken it upon themselves to create a situation in which an introduction is welcome. Because they have a clear understanding of one another's goals, it is also very easy to create Referral-Based Dating opportunities for each other, even if they don't happen to be together at the time.

In fact, it was Hank who introduced Laurie Sue to an old college friend he ran into, paving the way for what she considers one of the most enduring romances of her life.

The Dinner Party Technique

My friend Sydney and several of her girlfriends put their heads together and devised a terrific way to meet lots of eligible bachelors at once. Each invited seven or eight other women friends to a dinner party, and all the women were asked to bring one or more "attractive, eligible men with whom they are *not* personally involved." It was a potential win/win for everyone.

Sydney – who now happens to be happily married – stresses that women looking to meet new men should make sure to establish networking relationships with the right people...namely, other *women* who are in a position to set them up with the men they know. "The biggest mistake most women make is that they go to a party or event with the sole purpose of meeting and talking to *men*," says Sydney. "I've been introduced to more men by other *women* than I could ever have possibly met on my own!"

Sydney also points out that it's useful to expand your networking circle to people you would not ordinarily consider. "Meet *older* women!," she says. "They are usually more than happy to introduce their handsome sons and nephews, or their lovely daughters and nieces to someone who is eligible – namely, *you*. A good friend of mine contends that cultivating relationships with older women has been her most effective way of finding nice men to date."

It is possible for both women, and men, to create a unique arrangement in which you ask all your older female friends to consider introducing you to their relatives, friends and co-workers.

Sydney, in fact, is an excellent networker in her own right! I had the pleasure of reading a passage as part of the ceremony at her wedding. At the reception, she introduced me to two of her female friends. I sent each one a personal note immediately afterwards. One I have dated on several occasions and both are friends of mine to this day. That's one example of how networking can work during social occasions!

Throw A Theme Party

Theme parties are another unique way to bring people together to socialize and network.

Laurie Sue points out that some of the most interesting get-togethers of this nature include a "Come As You *Were*" party, in which participants dress up as people they wish they'd been in past lives; or a Halloween party in which everyone dresses up in a costume that represents a personal romantic ideal, such as Beast from *Beauty and the Beast*, or Scarlett O'Hara from *Gone With The Wind*.

These parties offer colorful, creative and visually stimulating opportunities to meet new people. You can easily wander over to "Sir Lancelot" and ask if he is indeed your knight in shining armor, or ask a friend to introduce you to "Marilyn Monroe."

There are any number of ways you can put together a theme-type party that can open a door to a myriad of romantic networking opportunities. They can be parties specifically for singles, or in which singles will have an opportunity to casually network for romantic possibilities in a dynamic social environment.

Every Effort Brings You Closer To Your Dream

If you don't meet the mate of your dreams at any of these kinds of gatherings, it doesn't matter. You will have a great time anyway, and you are that much closer to finding him or her because you'll have an opportunity to meet people of both genders with whom you can begin a networking relationship. Since you have met in a situation in which there is instant rapport – i.e., you are all clearly there for the same purpose – eventually one or more of these new friends may meet, and introduce you to, someone who could be just right for you!

Combining Entrepreneurship And Networking

Another interesting social networking idea comes from Caterina Rando, a "Success Coach" based in San Francisco. Along with another female entrepreneur, she created a party concept she calls "Renaissance Men" Parties. Caterina knew that personal ads would bring responses, but she was leery of the prospect of meeting a total stranger for a first date.

"The challenge for me was that going to meet a complete stranger for dinner was horrifying," she explains. "I knew I would be too shy, nervous, and self-conscious. But I asked myself how I could best utilize the ads without causing stress, and decided there had to be a way. That's how the 'Renaissance Men' parties were born."

She and her partner wrote an ad and placed it in a local paper. It read:

RENAISSANCE MEN WANTED
Young, successful, professional San Francisco women interested in arts, music, politics, culture, looking to meet men for cocktail party.

Did it work? "We got over 120 voice-mail responses," says Caterina. "We listened to each, weeded out the obvious crazies and gave not one but *four* cocktail parties!" Twenty-five men were invited to each event, and then Caterina and company went about "recruiting" single women to attend. They asked friends, friends of friends, and new networking contacts. The events were held at a plush Indian restaurant that had the perfect ambiance; a few trays of appetizers were purchased, and attendees paid for their own drinks.

"Everyone had a great time, and I personally had more dates

in the months that followed than I had in my whole preceding life," says Caterina. "These were men I would never have known if I had not made the effort to meet some new people. It was a real adventure. Besides new romance, I made many new friends and had fun! I was proud of myself for getting out there, taking a risk and making things happen. Instead of moping around and hoping for Prince Charmings to find me, I went out and found *them*!"

Another Uplifting Idea

Caterina is not the only person to use her business and entrepreneurial savvy to create a network for dating opportunities. In the same spirit, my friend Ann expanded her dating horizons when she developed a way to capitalize on an unusual aspect of her life.

An attractive woman in her late thirties, Ann happens to be extremely tall. When she moved to New York City she decided to call the National Tall Club, an organization for tall single people (men must be 6'4" or above and women 5'10" or above), and find out where the local chapter met. When she discovered that it didn't exist, she took it upon herself to start one.

"Between my chapter and the other chapters, my dating calendar has been as full as I want it to be," says Ann. "The referrals are great. Through this organization, I've had dates with men from as far away as Denmark."

It's amazing what some expanded thinking, creativity, and ingenuity can do for a person's social life. There are hundreds of special interest groups, similar in concept to The Tall Club, that might be appropriate for your needs. Looking in the Yellow Pages and joining one may be just the thing to start you on your path. If none exist in your community, or address your interests, imagine the power – and endless romance – that can be found by starting one of your own.

Business *And* Pleasure

Taking a course or professional training workshop can also lead to great networking opportunities in more ways than you might expect. Psychotherapist Joanna Poppink says she once attended a three-hour seminar designed to teach private practitioners like herself how to develop their public speaking skills. The class ended up being so dull that Joanna was one of only three people who stayed until the end. The "survivors" decided to network.

As they walked to the parking lot together, one of them told Joanna about a divorce attorney who was looking for a psychotherapist to team up with for public speaking engagements. Joanna, who had expertise in working with people impaired by divorce, thought this could be a promising business arrangement. She figured that her healing, personal growth and adult development stories might become part of a program that she and the divorce attorney could create together.

After getting the attorney's telephone number, she called and suggested lunch. Over the next several months, they continued to talk on the telephone, send notes, and meet often for lunch to discuss combining their talents on a program. Ultimately, this ended up creating more than a public speaking program!

As Joanna puts it, "He was a bright, generous, emotional and sensitive man. Gradually, our meetings turned into dates and a great personal relationship."

Be Creative, Have Fun and Help Others

Some of these ideas may be totally new to you, and others you might have heard before. All the people who contributed their stories to this chapter had several key things in common:

They were all single and "looking." They all understood that the true power of networking was to help others, and they learned that it was a natural result to also satisfy their own needs and desires. They all took the initiative to try something different in order to bring themselves closer to their chosen goals.

If that little voice – the one that says *I can't do this* – is talking to you again, you might find that one of the most powerful things that you can do, right now, this minute, is to talk back to it and say: *Yes, I can!*

PART THREE

♥

AVOIDING *R*ELATIONSHIP MALPRACTICE

Now that you've followed the techniques presented in this book, your dating calendar is filling up as you meet new people and begin to discover "who's out there." You might find it appropriate to update your Romantic Resumé with new discoveries. Perhaps you've decided the type you thought you were looking for is not the right type for the future you have in mind. Or maybe you have met that one special person: someone who has stolen your heart, with whom you're head over heels in love. This section addresses communication strategies for dating, as well as those that help you keep your flourishing relationship on track when your feet finally hit the ground! Both authors offer some thoughts on understanding romance, learning to communicate, recognizing real love and keeping the relationship you've worked so hard to find!

Chapter 10

from Laurie Sue's view:
The Anatomy of Referral-Based Romance

There's a Dating Evolution Going On!
There's a great line in a corny movie called *Masters of The Universe:* "Live the journey. Each destination is but a doorway to another. Good journey."

I believe that all of life is like that. But it's particularly potent when you apply it to dating: *"Live the dating experience. Each date is but a doorway to another. Good romantic journey."*

For those of you who approached this project as girls or guys *that just want to have fun*, then by all means you should be reveling in the opportunities for plenty of romantic interludes with quality people who – due to all your good work in clarifying the types of people you want to meet and networking to meet them – are the "right" dates. You may even find a slight shift in your desires: Perhaps along the way you've come to see that you do want to develop a special relationship, rather than dating many people.

Maybe you began this project with the sole intention of finding your soulmate... your other half, love of a lifetime, man/woman of your dreams. You've gone through the whole program, followed the steps, mastered the techniques, and now you're thinking: *Hello. Where are you, true love? The deal was you were supposed to be the prize at the end of the networking rainbow.*

At this point, you will find patience and the willingness to practice the art of romancing (and being romanced) are your greatest virtues because:

YOUR FIRST ROUND OF REFERRAL-BASED DATES MAY BE A TEST RUN FOR TRUE LOVE

Every time you go on a date you should be "assessing" the potential of the person you are with. That doesn't mean "judging" or harshly "evaluating" – it just means doing yet another reality check: *Is this person really right for me?* As Bob would say: Build on your small successes!

Baseball great Yogi Berra once said, "if you don't know where you're going you won't get there." That's so true. However, even though you have already done what it takes to make sure you are in the right "ball park" with the people you date, the dating period is the time to experiment and shift your playing strategy as needed.

Robert Fritz, a former teacher of mine, once told me that any vision, dream or goal may require a process of "create and adjust." For example, if your original vision was to marry a man who looks like actor Alec Baldwin, or a woman who resembles Pamela Anderson Lee, and you come to realize that you really don't care what a person looks like as long as he or she knows how to love you the way you want to be loved, then you would adjust the part of your vision – or Romantic Resumé – that specifies your mate has to be a specific physical type.

The only way to know for *sure* who is the most perfect mate for you is to get up to bat a few times in the dating arena.

Courting Your Way To Your Most Perfect Mate

Courtship was invented as a way for people to get to know one another and decide if they'd make a good match. It was supposed to be fun when so – and – so came "a-courtin'."

In the first half of the century, women went on short dates with a variety of men. And men often enjoyed "squiring" a number of females about to various activities. While *swooning* was permissible, *spooning* was not, so men and women relished simple pleasures together. Perhaps there was lunch, with Bernie, the butcher's son; a walk on the beach with Larry the lawyer; and dancing to big-band music in the park with Chuck the debonair musician. Those same men might take someone else in the neighborhood to another function that same day.

Unless you took the opportunity to check out the options, you might end up with the debonair musician, only to find you would have been better off with the butcher's son – and *not* just for the lifelong supply of steaks!

If you are someone who has a tendency to get emotionally involved very quickly with the first person who seems to come close to what you're looking for, this is a good time to give yourself permission to experiment and learn. Every relationship leads to the next and helps you grow. When your heart is set on finding someone special, taking even a few months to do more "research" may seem like an eternity. For my money, I'd say jumping into a relationship with the wrong person, and getting entangled, is the *real* eternity.

Some romances are short-lived, not meant to be more than a passing phase of your life – and a passageway to the next. For whatever reasons, they just can't or won't go any further than a few months or a few dates. While you of course want to be kind, respectful and honest with all the great people your networking friends have helped you meet, and you do not want to lead anyone on, if you find yourself in a relationship you *know* is not right for you, remember: there are plenty of Referral-Based Dates in the sea.

Compartmentalize Your Prospects

My friend Ted, who has learned the art of assessing people's dating potential in a short amount of time, tells me he finds it useful to compartmentalize people into certain categories. He calls it his "List." This could be a useful way to figure out where everyone you date fits into your personal picture and goals.

1. ***Brief, but sweet, romances:*** These occur between people who are not looking for a commitment. Both parties are in agreement from the start that the interactions are friendly and maybe even somewhat physical – and meant to be nothing more.
2. ***Occasional dates:*** These are for people who seem to hit it off and really like one another, yet are clear that they will see each other only from time to time. Lifestyles, schedules, location and goals may preclude this from going any further than a once-in-awhile date, but while you are "looking" they are great friends to know and have fun with.
3. ***Great prospects:*** These are people you just met, or have admired from afar, who for whatever reason you haven't yet dated. You sense that, when the time is right and you actually get together, something great could develop.
4. ***Could Be "The One":*** These are the people with whom you see the greatest potential for a monogamous, long-term relationship or marriage.

Dating Tips From The Female Viewpoint

Aside from the fact that I have interviewed THOUSANDS of men and women, as well as countless experts on topics of love, romance and sex, I have also, as they say, been around the block. I've lost count of how many times, but enough to assess some of my own dating blunders and offer some wisdom. This may be particularly useful to women who are clear that, ultimately, they want a committed relationship with the right person; yet men too can glean useful insights from these tips. As you gallivant about and have fun, do so with the intent of being smart romantic "consumers."

1. Start out with casual dates in neutral environments.
Obviously, if a man invites you for a short flight in his private plane or to breakfast in Paris, *you may want to go just for the experience.* That type of "candlelight dinners and moonlit walks on the beach" date is a favorite female fantasy, and such dates are indeed romantic. But they're also deceiving, because what you are experiencing is the fantasy without yet assessing the reality. If you can bear it, stay away from anything too seductive for the first date — and the few that follow — so you can really get to know who a guy is before you get swept away. The part of you that longs for amorous adventure may be utterly seduced by romantic, sexy environments. *Anyone* can look like "the one" on a moonlit beach, especially after a candle-lit dinner and a few sips of wine!

2) Don't tell everything about yourself at first.
Bob has given you some fabulous "you-oriented" questions and techniques...*use* them! While you want to be genuine and open, you don't want to blurt out your entire life story on day one. If you, like the person I look at in the mirror every morning, long to "share", consider dishing information out in a totally new manner — slowly! First off, men are the natural "fixers" of the

universe, and if you tell him too much about your life challenges, he is going to feel compelled to have to "fix things" for you – and he may not yet feel up to the job. You may not even *want* him to fix anything, you may just be "sharing"; he, however, will likely hear it as a call to action. As a relationship grows, of course it will be his natural instinct, as it will be yours, to reach out and help. In general, it's been my experience, that most men – not all, but most – will opt for mystery over true confessions, at least not at first. Communicating who you really are is a process that deserves an adequate amount of time to unfold.

3) Get the hang of male-female communications.
I don't care what anyone says: Men and women, more often than not, speak a different language and process information differently. As pointed out before, sociolinguistics specialist Deborah Tannen, Ph.D. calls it "cross-cultural communication." I am often TOTALLY AWED by the fact that a woman can say something to a man and by the time it has gone through his ears to his brain it's been translated into something with a completely different meaning. It's like getting a Macintosh to read a PC file; you've got to turn it into "simple text" or the systems cannot speak a common language. We all have to take responsibility for learning one another's native tongue. It will give you the edge on communication and help you figure out where a guy is really coming from – *if* you translate into guy language.

4) Don't tell him about all the other people you're dating
Just don't. While there may come a time in which the relationship gets more serious and it's necessary to make a joint decision about whether or not you both want a monogamous union,

that time is not now. Even when it does role around, be cautious – there's a thin line between being honest and simply offering too many details. While a man can be turned on by the fact that a woman is popular and sought-after, he will hate the thought that you are sizing him up and comparing him to others. Although he probably figures you're seeing other people, he doesn't really want to bring that factor into his relationship with you – yet.

5) Pay attention!!

Infatuation does wild and wonderful things to the mind and body. It can also make you clueless about what's *real* and what's a *fantasy* you are projecting. It's natural to feel hopeful and to hope he is "the one." Yet when you lose perspective there is a tendency to not pay attention to certain clues. For example, if a guy is gorgeous, charming or seems to be wealthy, and you are taken by those particular types of qualities, you may totally miss it when he drops those subtle little hints. For example, he may look great on the outside and exude the kind of charm you go for, yet, he has this little tendency to be nasty to servers, aggressive and loud when he drives and, whoa, he's forgotten his wallet on the last three dates you've had with him! A dramatic example, but you get the point: There is a big difference between accepting the faults of someone you love and ignoring any bad behavior on the part of a person you are afraid of losing. Just be aware of his style and behavior and see if it really meshes and matches with your goals.

You might want to create a few personal romance "litmus tests". Sex educator Sari Locker told me she tells men right off the bat that flowers are a very important gesture to her. If a guy doesn't send any after the first few dates, he's out. For me, it's the day after, what-a-great-time-I-had call that's one of the ways I gauge, personally, how important I am to a man.

6) Stop falling in love with potential.
We all have to cut this out. I think women in particular have a genetic disposition and need to change men and an uncanny tendency to fall in love with a man's "potential." Men complain about that constantly; they hate it and resist it. As Sydney Biddle Barrows says, what a man hears when a woman wants to change him is "you're not good enough the way you are" – even if all the woman wants to do is get rid of his awful wardrobe.

Two points: 1) In the natural flow of love, people often influence and transform another, if only by mirroring back one another's finest points and inspiring one another to grow – i.e., if it doesn't happen naturally, it ain't going to happen; 2) Potential *is* potential. It's not "some day he'll change," it's "I hope he changes some day." Trying to change a unique individual into something he has not yet become is an impossible task that women constantly take on in relationships.

A *boyfriend* I once tried to change gave me this wise advice: "What you see is what you get" and "always take a man at his word." If a guy says he doesn't want marriage, or children, believe him; if he says he'll never wear jeans, he's going to feel that you're turning him into your own personal Ken doll if you buy him a pair.

7) Have fun.
Some of the most dynamic, independent, successful women I know lose their sense of humor when they start getting serious too soon about a man. It's as if there is a short window of

opportunity in which you can take him or leave him, and then, suddenly, you are past the point of no return. Like the character in Erica Jong's *Any Woman's Blues*, women often turn into love junkies waiting by the phone. *Hello.* We've all been there once or twice – or more – and maybe this is a good time to pass on romantic drama. If you find yourself obsessing over what a man is thinking, doing and feeling, you are stepping into co-dependent territory and it may be time for another reality check. If you are in misery about a particular man most of the time, it could be that he is simply not the one who will provide the source of nourishment you seek in a loving partner. If you still can't seem to shake the "addiction" to a guy, ask yourself: *Do I really want to live like this?*

Identifying The Real Mr./Ms. Right – Tactfully, Of Course!

I've said it before, I'll say it again: Don't give up on your project before you get to your goal. This is *your* life, and *your* dream – you truly deserve to exercise the right to create your own romantic destiny! So, during your stint of casual dating, take the time to clarify, reclarify and clarify again who would be the most perfect mate.

Since this may require dating your way through a number of people who, however wonderful, are not wonderful for you in the long run, you have to find a way to move on from those who are inappropriate. You don't want to figure it out a few months after you marry the person – trust me on that!

You also don't want to be hurtful, insulting or rude to any of the nice people you meet. Your best solution may be the one that fits right into your networking plan – pass him or her along to a friend! It may sound harsh, but think of it this way: You have already done the research of finding out enough about a person to know that this is not a person for you. But he or she might be a sure fit for a friend, one you are actively networking with or someone you happen to know.

Although few people relish the thought of hearing "I like you a lot, but..." sometimes it is the only way to prevent what could turn into a sticky situation. If you've started out slowly and kept as much emotional distance as possible, it is easier to cut a relationship off before it's roots are implanted in your life.

Remember, this is a business-like approach to dating, and just as in business, if a person is not right for the position, it would be a bad move for all concerned to prolong their stay.

Men have often confided to me that a man would much rather be dropped from the game before he expends a lot of emotional energy on a woman in an unproductive way. A guy would rather be "selected out" up front than have his heart broken and his pride wounded.

I once went out on two dates with a man who I really, really liked, yet I sensed that something wasn't clicking. We had become friends, we had fun together, but there was no spark. Although it stung at first, I was ultimately relieved when he called and said: "You're a great person and I enjoy your company, and I really think we should keep this platonic." He went on to become one of my best friends.

A Time For Love

When I was younger, and my friends began to get married, it was difficult to comprehend how they were able to come to such a huge, life-changing decision. I'd always ask: "How did you know he/she was the right person?" And I'd inevitably hear, "I just knew."

Now I'm convinced that the way that many people arrive at

"just knowing" is by defining, in their minds, before hand, who the right person is – so that they'd "recognize" that person when he or she comes around.

That's exactly what you've been doing, and now it's up to you to let your instincts guide you.

When you know the person you are dating is truly the one for you, it is one of the most exquisite feelings on the planet. Everything is filled with promise, passion and possibility. You think of him or her constantly, call every chance you get, see each other as much as possible. You can't get that person out of your mind. You are literally engulfed by the flames of romantic passion.

Sexologist Patti Britton, Ph.D., labels this head-over-heels-in-love feeling "limerence." It is the state of "in-loveness" and in the average relationship it lasts between three weeks and three months. I call it the "grace period."

While it is totally possible to fall in love – for real – during that stage, it is also totally possible to think you've fallen out of love when, suddenly, your feet hit the ground and the first burst of passionate love begins to lose intensity. Without the excitement of the initial stages, you get to the *next* level of knowing who a person is. It's a period that really tests your love, and makes or breaks a relationship. It is possible to lift off, from this point, to greater intimacy; a place where you can truly share yourself, and life, with a partner who is there, who cares, and who intends to stay. The tricky part is you miss the "thrill," and some people interpret this as "the thrill is gone" – forever. It's so important to recognize that relationships are growing, evolving organisms, and that, just as you water plants every morning, you've got to tend a relationship and make sure it too keeps growing.

In his classic novel *Still Life With Woodpecker*, author Tom Robbins let his character, the Princess Leigh-Cheri, sum it up this way: "We waste time looking for the perfect lover instead of creating the perfect love. Wouldn't that be the way to make love stay?"

Even though you have put much effort into your search for the mate of your dreams, you have probably discovered by now that this is not a person whom you can construct by making a particular individual change to suit your needs. More likely, you have come to realize you must *seek out an appropriate individual with whom you can create the perfect love relationship* – a happy, fulfilling, loving, healthy, stimulating union that lasts.

One of life's biggest challenges is to bring two unique and multi-faceted individuals together to form a unified couple. For most people, it is not a matter of continuing to love; it is a matter of continuing to *fall in love* and *be in love* with the person they've chosen as a mate.

In the next chapter, Bob offers some beautiful and positive insights into communication strategies that will get you through the "honeymoon period"...and way beyond.

Chapter 11

from Bob's view:
How To Avoid "Relationship Malpractice"
Effective Communication Is The Key To Endless Romance

Two people who are committed to being givers possess the basic tools for fostering deep love and a sense of intense oneness.
– NACHUM BRAVERMAN and SHIMON APISDORF
From **The Death of Cupid**

In the early stages of love, people often go out of their way to romance and communicate with the person who has won their heart. Then, when the "honeymoon period" is over, they aren't sure how to properly nourish the relationship. Some even seem to lose the desire to keep the doors to communication open. I believe that by implementing some very basic measures of thoughtful communication, you can help love to flourish long after the first fires of romantic passion fade.

As Laurie Sue pointed out, the moment the excitement *fizzles* some couples believe it's the first cue that a relationship is over. How many times in your life, and in your friends' and family's, have you watched a potentially great relationship die? Perhaps it's the caring communication that brought them together in the first place that has died – not the love. The following information is devoted to strengthening effective communication – and illustrating how it can make your relationship continue to flourish.

"Servicing The Sale"

A natural instinct in the initial stages of love is to want to make the other person happy. As people grow more accustom to having someone in their lives, they tend to forget that any relationship requires ongoing maintenance. In business, the art of keeping the customer or client happy is called "servicing the sale." A good salesperson can do, and usually does, everything right from the "courting period" to successfully "closing the sale." But in order to keep that business, it's crucial to nurture the relationship and keep the lines of effective communication open. In other words, the sale doesn't end just because the transaction has been completed.

Well, the exact same principle applies to romance. As unromantic as it may sound, it is crucial to continue servicing the sale. You probably already know from experience that the greatest pitfall in any relationship is when you stop doing what it takes to keep it alive. Many people do not have a clue what's required to nurture a romantic union. After all, we live in a country with a 50 percent divorce rate – need I say more?

The High Cost of Relationship Malpractice

I believe the major reason for failed marriages is malpractice... "Relationship Malpractice," that is. Let me explain: If you go to a doctor and he or she gives a diagnosis and prescription without first asking your symptoms, or knowing your medical history, that might constitute medical malpractice. Hence, if you were to try to communicate with your spouse without finding out what he or she needed, or where he or she is coming from, that could be Relationship Malpractice.

Regardless of the numerous years of education and vast amount of knowledge a physician has in medicine, it would be difficult to even attempt to make a diagnosis and suggest a particular treatment without more data, from the patient directly and through tests. The doctor must first "listen" for information.

Similarly, in our relationships, actively listening to a partner, we gather important information. What do they feel? How do they feel? Why do they feel that way? What is working in their life and what isn't? What do they perceive to be life's truths? If you don't take the time to ask, listen and learn, you may never know. The high cost of Relationship Malpractice may be the emotional bankruptcy of your relationship.

Six "Magical Ingredients" For Effective Relationship Communication

There is no dearth of relationship manuals in the market place today. Books, audio tapes, videos and courses on dating, romance, compatibility, marriage and love abound. Many of the resources are excellent. I encourage you to seek out whatever information will help you to grow, and to utilize whatever tips work for you, applying them with those you've learned in this book. Take the best from the best, and *become* the best relationship partner you can be.

What you want to avoid in any relationship is the kind of miscommunication that lead to what was just described as "Relationship Malpractice." The following is my personal interpretation of the communication skills and ingredients that will help you on your quest, and ensure the delicious outcome you desire.

I've shown you how to network your way to endless romance, and now I want to offer you my heartfelt view on how you can keep and strengthen the love you worked so hard to find!

1. *Truth*
It's important to realize that while honesty is essential to a good

relationship, the term "truth," in this scenerio, is relative to the personal perceptions of each individual in that relationship. Simply put: What one person might perceive to be the truth (the "correct" way of doing things) is not necessarily what their partner perceives to be the truth.

You may perceive an event, thing, situation, or way of handling something as "the right way," yet your way may not match the perceptions of your significant other. That doesn't mean that person is wrong. It also doesn't mean that you are wrong. It means that particular instance *you just don't see eye to eye*. What often happens when couples disagree is they argue or go around in endless circles of high-volume conversation. While some people do attempt to reach an agreement through compromise, others simply work at trying to change the other's mind.

Typically, when the parties don't get what they want or come to a satisfactory conclusion, they continue their yelling match, or else they withdraw altogether. Obviously, everyone has to let off steam and express anger now and then; and studies have shown that couples who know how to have *productive* disagreements have healthier unions. But when you find yourself trading nasty comments and attacking one another...NOBODY WINS! Instead, one or both of you will feel wounded, bitter or hurt. This can literally kill a relationship that might otherwise thrive.

Although you might perceive a trying moment with your significant other as a big fight, I encourage you to look at it different way – as a BIG MISCOMMUNICATION. The best thing you can do to lessen the odds of miscommunication is to communicate... effectively.

It doesn't just mean talking: It means learning to truly listen to your partner and discover where that person is coming from.

That requires *active* listening – not just "hearing," but being interested, empathetic and responsive. Put yourself in the other person's shoes. Why is *their* version of the truth, or their correct way of doing things, so important to that individual that he or she feels they must fight for it? What is it in that person's upbringing and past that has painted their world view? What do you need to know about your mate in order to understand that mate's perspective?

You simply won't know some of these things until you ask. This is where your "you-oriented" approach is again a powerful tool to creating rapport. While you have to respect your own feelings of anger and upset, and need the chance to say your piece, practice listening to your loved one and trying to understand. As much as you may feel compelled to chime in and interrupt, do your best not to: It can evoke in the other person even greater feelings of frustration, anger and despair.

In a wonderful book called *The Death of Cupid: Reclaiming the Wisdom of Love, Dating, Romance and Marriage*, authors Nachum Braverman and Shimon Apisdorf point out: "There [also] exists another dimension to listening that Jewish wisdom calls *sharing the load*. Sharing the load means to identify with someone else's burdens, to be troubled by his or her troubles."

This does not mean that you are expected to become a receptacle for another's hostilities and abuse. It does mean that if the health of your relationship matters to you, you must be willing to hear your partner's pain with an empathetic ear. Striving to understand the pain of the person you care for, and helping that person through, means a willingness to understand their truth, as they see it.

Some people approach romantic miscommunications from such an adversarial point of view that there is no room for people to express the burdens that trigger their reactions in the first place. You have a much better chance of succeeding if, rather than acting like a lawyer who is trying to win a case, you behave like a true partner, attempting to negotiate a win/win situation.

My friend and fellow author Jim Cathcart talks about the difference between the Golden Rule and the Platinum Rule. The Golden Rule, of course, is, "Do unto others as you would have them do unto you." The Platinum Rule, according to Jim, is, "Do unto others as *they* want to be done unto."

That, to me, is the difference between an individual insisting on their partner seeing the truth exactly as they see it, and being willing to see the truth from their partner's point of view. When you are willing to do that for them, a truly caring partner will work on doing the same for you.

Take Tom and Janet, for instance, a couple who had been in a relationship for a relatively short period of time before realizing that their "truths" regarding problem solving were based on diametrically opposite styles. Tom's family members were communicators and problem-solvers. When the first signs of a problem arose between two or more family members, immediately it was brought out into the open, worked on in a mature fashion, and ultimately solved. This is one way Tom's family expressed their love and respect for one another.

Janet's family, on the other hand, when a problem surfaced, would either initially sweep it right under the carpet, or yell and scream, never actually communicating. Their conflicts were never truly resolved, and the result was that *the same problems would resurface over and over.*

Tom and Janet finally opted to rectify their situation by going to counseling, learning to understand the cause of their conflict (their individual styles of "truth" when problem-solving), and working on a way to see the truth from each other's point of view.

2. *Justice*

Justice, again, is a relative term. Yet the principle involves being mature enough to admit "Hey, I'm wrong" when you are. Even though couples may come at truth from different perspectives, that doesn't mean that acting inappropriately or irresponsibly is unconditionally acceptable. Justice means to find the balance and admit when you are the one who has thrown that balance off by something you've said, you've done or *have not done*. It requires taking responsibility to say "I can, and *will* do something about it. I *will* change the behavior that is destructive to our relationship."

For some people, admitting to being the source of a miscommunication or painful situation is the hardest thing in the world. As a result, many people allow love to perish in their need to be *right* and clear of any blame. You can't even hope to communicate effectively with someone who finds it impossible to acknowledge when they are wrong. The partner who tries to is almost always faced with an impenetrable wall.

Confrontations occur and reoccur again and again because of the inability to admit shortcomings, when admitting those shortcomings actually serves to make you a greater hero in your partner's eyes.

Look at justice from the viewpoint of Tom and Janet. Janet thinks that the way Tom's family solves problems is a better way than her family's. She now feels as though she can say to Tom, "I'm not sure how easy it will be for me to adjust, based on how I've been brought up. However, I'd like to try to communicate better when we have disagreements."

Tom is touched by Janet's willingness to even consider that her approach isn't the most beneficial. "I really appreciate your saying that and my love for you is even stronger when I know you're willing to do whatever it takes to make our relationship better. There are certainly plenty of areas where I know I need to adjust *my* thinking in order to more effectively meet *your* needs."

That is justice in communication.

3. *Peace*

Everyone needs, and deserves, peace in their lives. And no one can live a peaceful life if they are in a primary relationship in which they feel they must always walk on eggshells or watch every word they say for fear of starting a confrontation.

In general, peace in one's relationship, and hence in one's life, seems to come about when there is comfort and little stress in dealing with each other. It's a feeling of easiness that comes from feeling "at home" with your partner.

In the best of situations, you and your mate are not afraid to say things to each other. You're not under pressure because if there is any kind of misunderstanding about the truth, the two of you will be able to work it out. More than anything else, peace results from two people sharing a mutual respect and friendship.

By consciously working at bringing peace back to their relationship, Tom and Janet have a new sense of security and comfort. They now know it is not a matter of being right or wrong, but more a matter of: "How do we learn from this situation?" In other words, they are no longer taking on the role of adversaries, but that of friends and teammates in order to grow together.

4. *Love*

I believe this means, simply, putting your partner ahead of yourself. To my mind, the only way you can achieve and maintain true love is to make the needs and desires of your significant other even more important than your own. I know there are people who would strongly disagree and perhaps say that's not possible in "the real world." However, having been fortunate enough to be raised in a family with parents who were, and still are, truly equal partners and best friends, I learned this is in fact *absolutely* "real."

While growing up, I often noticed that my parents thrived on their love and concern for one another. That doesn't mean that their relationship didn't take work – everything of value in life does – but it proves that this kind of devoted love is actually possible. Even if you don't come from the same kind of background, you can *create* this as a truth in and for your own married life.

I know it is popular in this culture to toss around phrases such as "You come first" and "Do what's best for you, and then worry about someone else." However, in my observation, couples in which each partner cares more about the other than about himself or herself have the happiest and most fulfilling relationships.

PLEASE NOTE: I AM ABSOLUTELY *NOT* TALKING ABOUT ABUSIVE OR CO-DEPENDENT RELATIONSHIPS. For someone who is in a co-dependent or abusive relationship, where all that individual does is take care of another's needs and put up with abuse, continuing to put the needs of that person before their own is self-destructive. In a case like that, the needs and demands of the abusive partner are unfair and damaging.

I'm talking about a relationship between two equal partners based on genuine caring and emotional maturity. Put that other person ahead of yourself, and love will be returned...and you'll return that...and then they'll return it back to you. It becomes a natural way of being...a continuing cycle of relationship success.

As Tom and Janet grow together in their natural process of giving to one another and receiving all that each has to give, each is even more anxious and devoted to pleasing the other. In their relationship as lovers and friends, they are realizing that their love is a mutual win/win situation, not a power struggle. They know the main objective of each is to make the other happier. They have discovered that happiness begets happiness and that happy partners make for a happy union. Even though this may sound Pollyanna-ish, the truth is, when you love and respect someone at a mature level, it gives great satisfaction to know that the other person feels and appreciates how much you want to do for them.

5. *Edification*

According to Webster's, "to edify" means to build. Put into the vernacular of everyday life, to edify someone means to *build* them up verbally. Generally speaking, when we think of edifying, or "bragging about someone," we put it in the context of telling others. We speak of our partner to others in only the nicest and most complimentary terms, saying how terrific, smart, attractive, etc. our significant other is. I believe that's a wonderful policy to employ; in doing so, you also continue to boost your own appreciation of that very special person.

If we publicly edify our significant other, when they are not present, we are truly honoring them. When we edify them *in* their presence, they are proud to be with us, proud of being a part of our lives. And even if we are edifying based on positive traits they might not at present possess, they'll make a point to work harder to live up to that "great press."

But what about edifying that person to his or her face – second-person singular? What about bragging on them *to* them, complimenting them, telling them often about the things they do so well, how great they make you feel? When you consistently acknowledge a partner's finest qualities it empowers them completely, and only adds to their confidence and self esteem. Then that partner brings all those wonderful attributes back into the relationship.

How often does an otherwise loving partner say to a third party, "I don't have to say how much I love my partner, he/she already knows!" Consider this: *They need to hear it anyway!* There is an added bonus: If you want to create or build a particular strength or quality in your significant other, you can do this by treating them as if they already possess it. Constantly edify them for already having that quality, and in time, they'll aquire it.

That's a lot more effective than saying, *Why don't you do this? How come you never . . . ?* Instead, tactfully work into a conversation how you love it when they _____. Or you really appreciate it when they _____. Warning: Please do not think that this method doesn't work just because after trying it twice you don't see concrete results. Stay consistent, and in time you'll begin to see positive changes.

And while we are on the topic of "second person singular edification," don't *ever* compare your partner with someone else. (Especially not with the partner of a friend of yours.) Virtually nothing in the world will destroy the confidence and self-esteem of a person more than being compared to someone who exhibits attributes you desire in a mate.

And, of course, you realize that when you edify your partner, he or she will most likely begin edifying you even more!

Tom and Janet continually edify each other, both to outsiders and to one another. And the edification they now display to each other is in more than just words. It's the kisses for no particular reason, the touches on the shoulder, the spontaneous hugs. The comfortable silences between them. They display such genuine caring for each other that when one does need to offer constructive criticism, the other will never take it the wrong way. That's the power of edification!

6. *Tact*

So, so important! Tact is "the language of strength." If we could listen on tape to what we say in everyday conversations, we'd be amazed at our lack of tact and sensitivity in the way we relate to others. And, when it comes to those we care about, it's often even worse. In our comfort zone, we tend to think less about what we say and how we say it, which is counter to successfully expressing the loving and caring feelings to our partner we want to communicate.

A good friend of mine says that you can call someone the "worst name in the book," but if you say it with the right words and feeling (tact), they'll thank you for it! And I've seen him do it. He's a master, and he's worked hard at perfecting that skill. Well, my friend may have more guts than I have, but from personal experience I can vouch for the fact that anything said with the right amount of tact will work significantly better and be more persuasive than the alternative.

There's a great deal of truth in the old saying, "You can catch more flies with honey than you can with vinegar." Make an agreement with yourself to analyze the way you talk to your partner for just 21 days. Note your improvement every day and be proud of yourself.

When Janet does need to offer constructive criticism to Tom, she's aware that the best method is to precede the suggestion with a sincere compliment. An approach lacking in tact might be, "Tom, you were supposed to pick up the dry cleaning and you forgot it!" Instead, she may tactfully say, "Honey, you're always so terrific about picking up the dry cleaning. I would really appreciate your letting me know if something comes up that prevents you from doing it."

7. The "I Message"

This is not to be confused with being "I-oriented." In Chapter Six we covered the fact that when meeting someone new, we need to be "you-oriented" as opposed to "I-oriented." This means we focus our attention on the other person, investing 99.9% of the conversation asking that person questions about themselves, their life, their business, etc.. We ask how we can know if someone we're talking to would be a good prospect or contact for *them*. Being "you-oriented" will certainly help in establishing a win/win relationship.

The "I message," however, is something totally different. This is where we put the onus of a challenge or misunderstanding upon ourselves, taking the other person off the hook, making them more receptive to finding a solution to the challenge. We saw an example of the "I message" in the previous example under tact. When Janet gave Tom the "I message," putting the focus on *her* ("I really appreciate..."), she was certainly employing tact.

The "you message" would put the blame on the *other* person, making them defensive and less receptive to a win/win outcome. Master the "I message"; you'll be surprised to see less defensiveness during discussions and disagreements.

Let's look at still another example involving our friends Tom and Janet. While they were discussing a point, Tom began to speak to Janet in a somewhat sarcastic tone. The consideration and respect he usually showed her was missing at that particular moment.

Instead of saying to Tom, "*You're* talking down to me and not showing me respect" (that of course is a "you message," as in, you are at fault), she said, "Tom, *I'm* feeling upset. It might just be how

I'm taking it, but it feels as though I'm being put down and not being shown the respect that you usually show me." What she did was utilize the "I message" technique. In this way, Janet got her point across loud and clear that he was not speaking appropriately *and* Tom did not feel the need to *react* defensively.

In his book *How To Argue And Win Every Time*, famed attorney Gerry Spence points out the importance of phrasing a statement which ties right in with the "I message." For instance, he suggests the "I message" – "I feel upset" – as opposed to the "You message" – "You upset me." "I feel cheated" is an "I message" instead of the "you message," "You cheated me."

The author-attorney related how he might let a judge know he feels the judge is not treating him fairly. He'd never send out a "you message" such as "You are unfair" or "You are being rude to me." Instead he would use an "I message" such as, "Judge, I feel helpless." And then go on to explain his plight. Yes, the "I message" takes some practice, but in the end it will prove to be a very worthwhile and effective communication skill.

Are You A Parent, Adult Or Child?

In the best-selling book *Games People Play*, author Eric Berne, often credited with being the father of Transactional Analysis, points out three distinct personality states: *Parent, Adult,* and *Child.* These are states displayed by each of us, depending upon what we are feeling at any particular time. The following is my interpretation of these three states and how they relate to the nurturing of a relationship.

The Child in all of us is the perceived victim. He or she feels like a baby – put down, blamed, punished, controlled. As a result, a person in that state is angry and looking to get even. And usually the Child wants to get even with the person who assumes the Parent role.

The Parent in all of us is usually a victim of upbringing, biases and environment. People in the Parent role criticize, put others down, attempt to control. They mean well; they just don't recognize negative communication. They don't realize that they're putting somebody down. They don't realize that they're making somebody feel bad.

The Adult in all of us, which is the ideal, is the positive negotiator, the communicator – the respectful, honest, active listener who's trustworthy and just. And somebody who's easy to love.

Isn't it true that we play all three of these roles within a relationship? When our partner criticizes, condemns, or otherwise talks down to us, they are acting as the Parent and we are the Child. When this occurs we shouldn't take it personally (as difficult as that may be), but instead realize that we have to bring ourselves up to the Adult level in order to effectively deal with the situation.

We should also make sure we don't come across like the Parent talking down to our partner, putting them in the position of the Child.

Ideally, we want every transaction with our significant other to be on the level of adult to adult. It may not be easy, but it's possible with awareness, practice, and work.

It's also important to keep this in mind: You can't expect your partner to immediately grasp this concept just because *you* know what you're trying to accomplish. So don't feel put down if at first it's not working 100%. Again, reaching an adult-to-adult level of conversation on a consistent basis takes time and effort. But you can do it. Even if you get frustrated, keep working at it – the rewards can be bountiful.

Be aware the next time you are in a transaction that is *not* adult-to-adult, and see if you can work towards a win/win outcome. Do this by *building* that person up to an adult level, in order to match your level. As always, keep building on your small successes and you will find that baby steps will turn to giant strides; the child will eventually become an adult!

The Five Questions Of Life

A post Biblical sage by the name of Simeon ben Zoma shared his philosophy about different states of being in the form of four basic questions and answers. My dad later (as in thousands of years later!) added a fifth question and answer. I'd like to relate all five and ask you to read them also with an eye toward using them to increase the happiness in your relationships.

Question 1: *Who is a Wise Person?*

ben Zoma's answer to this first question was, "One who learns from others."

How many famous quotes and sayings paraphrase that philosophy? For example, "We have two ears and only one mouth for a reason." When we talk, we must be saying something that we either already know, or think we know. How can we become wiser doing that? Only by listening can we become wiser in our life and thus our relationships. As we learn our partner's expressed needs, we can become wiser about what direction to take to fulfill them.

Question 2: *Who is a Mighty Person?*

According to ben Zoma the answer is, "One who can control his or her emotions, and make, of an enemy, a friend."

This means having enough self-control and discipline to take a potentially negative situation and make it work *for* you. Let's apply this concept to your relationship.

When you put yourself in the Adult mindset, which often takes real effort during the heat of an emotionally difficult moment; when you *can* control your emotions you are in a much better position to take a lemon of a situation and turn it into lemonade.

As angry as Kent made Molly during an argument by bringing up past mistakes of hers from years ago, Molly refused to give in to temptation and do the same thing to him. Instead, she took a moment to think, and then calmly reminded him that bringing up the past was contrary to a very sacred agreement they made with each other. By remaining in control of herself, she was mighty and he responded in a positive way.

The person who practices self-control consistently is indeed a mighty person. As you master this ability through work and practice (who ever said bliss was supposed to be easy?) you'll strengthen your relationship more and more. The results will be habit-forming.

Question 3: *Who is a Rich Person?*
ben Zoma said, "A rich person is one who appreciates his or her lot."

In other words, a "rich person" is happy with his or her life, lifestyle, personal relationships, etc., feeling complete and truly content.

As you might expect, the usual response to that question is "Someone who has money." Certainly there's nothing wrong with having money. It's just that money, in and of itself, can only make a person wealthy. It can't make one "rich" in life's other blessings, and certainly not in the spirit of ben Zoma's definition.

Even if your situation right now is not exactly what you want it to be, that doesn't mean you aren't rich. If you can appreciate not only where you are now but where you are heading, and if you are prepared to do what it takes to get there, you *are* rich. Think rich, imagine yourself that way, and you will soon *be* that way – rich in happiness, and then, more than likely, financially as well.

Question 4: *Who is an Honored Person?*
According to ben Zoma, "One who honors others." One who makes *others* feel good is himself or herself an honored person. Let's go back to edification: openly and without qualification showing your appreciation to your partner. It's a formula that has proven its value and has most definitely withstood the test of time. Honor your partner and you will become honored.

Question 5: *Who is a Brave Person?*
"One who is smart enough to be afraid and still do their job." This question and answer was proposed by my Dad, himself a "wise, mighty, rich, honored and brave" person. Of course, in the context of personal relationships, the words "do their job" could easily be substituted with "go forward in order to make the situation work."

There are people who, although they are always willing to go into battle and put themselves on the line (as in war, business, etc.), are not necessarily brave because they are not scared. Maybe they don't have a reason to be. Maybe they don't know enough to be scared.

While you have to give those people credit for what they do, it's the person who acknowledges feelings about being scared and goes ahead anyway, trying to accomplish what he or she set out to do, who deserves the real pat on the back.

Please be assured that being scared is not the same as being cowardly or weak. Acknowledging that you are afraid when it is appropriate to be, is acknowledging true feelings. Being brave means taking action in doing the right thing, *despite* the fear. Someone once said, "Bravery is not the absence of fear, but the mastery of it."

How does that relate to a one-on-one relationship? Okay, let's say that you're the one recognizing there are problems between the two of you, but your partner is in denial. Thus *you* must take full responsibility to do what's necessary in order to save the relationship. That's scary! But if you've decided it's worth it, then you'll proceed despite all your fears and trepidations. That's courage! That's bravery!

Throughout this chapter we've taken basic principles of success in communication and applied them to personal relationships. These principles can be used in all aspects of your life, not only with your significant other, but also with family, friends, associates and practically anyone else.

Good communication takes work. I've given you my guidelines for effective communication, but you must do your job and practice them. I want your relationships to be happy, healthy, and long-lasting!

PART FOUR

♥

YOUR CONTINUED $\mathscr{S}$ UCCESS

*How to Keep Yourself
On Track With
"The Road Map To Success"*

In Closing...
Chapter 12

Keep Yourself On Track
Continue To Follow The Road Map To Success

It is one of the most beautiful compensations of life that no one can sincerely try to help another without helping him or herself.
– **RALPH WALDO EMERSON**

Something that truly fascinates me is the fact that those people who give the most of themselves for the benefit of others always seem to be repaid many times over in life. What fascinates me even more is how many people still refuse to believe that "niceness" can equal "winning" in this culture.

People have a tendency to use skills of war and aggression in their everyday life, when they could significantly reduce stress and constantly contribute to a better world if only they didn't buy into the saying, "Nice guys (and gals) finish last."

That saying has always bothered me because it just not true. Nice people finish first. It may take nice, giving, caring people a bit longer to accomplish their goals and they may have to work harder; but success, when attained the *right* way, sticks like glue. The right way, in my mind, is to proceed with good will, honesty, integrity and communication.

Don't get me wrong: It isn't that some people who happen to be nice don't get taken advantage of sometimes; but that doesn't necessarily have anything to do with their being nice. We need to be careful not to confuse niceness with weakness. Being nice does not mean allowing oneself to be taken advantage of or subjected to abuse. That's called being a "martyr." Martyrs, in general, are proud of their situation, and seem to get an unhealthy thrill from it. Typically, martyrs don't find true happiness. After all, if they did find happiness, how could they maintain their position as martyrs?

Being a nice person does not mean sitting back and waiting for life to happen. It is everyone's birthright to do whatever it takes to make their dreams come true; nice people simply make sure their tactics are legal, ethical, moral and of benefit to all concerned.

You Too Can Change Your Life!

For many years I labored under a self-imposed, and absolutely incorrect rule: In order to be a true success, I had to accomplish everything without the help, advice and wisdom of others. I somehow reasoned that it was "cheating" to learn from other people's experiences and felt, instead, I could only learn through my own mistakes. Imagine the frustration of my loving parents, who had so much wisdom to share, seeing their son struggle financially and flounder emotionally.

Finally, one day, I woke up...and realized my erroneous thinking was getting me NOWHERE, FAST! As the saying goes, "I was sick and tired of being sick and tired." I decided to do something about it; to take action. From that point on, I became a sponge for knowledge, a human vacuum cleaner taking up any strand of useful, insightful information I could find. As a result, I've learned that while there is no magic pill that will take us from point A to Z instantaneously, the "road map to success" will eventually lead us to any chosen destination. More importantly, it will keep us on track as we hit the curves, bumps and winding roads of life.

What I term "The Road Map To Success" is not particularly

lengthy, brilliant or difficult to understand. It is simple to apply but not always *easy*. Think about it: There can be a big difference between *simple* and *easy*. However, if you follow this road map consistently – sticking with it, without expectation of "instant results" – you will find that you can accomplish pretty much anything you set out to do...Whether it be to increase your social and romantic opportunities or to improve any other area of your life. Keep in mind, engaging in any life-enhancing activity will add power to your mission to find the mate of your dreams!

Here Is Your Road Map

There are basically three principles involved in The Road Map To Success.

Principle Number 1: *Seek out and find the road map in the first place.*

In other words, acknowledge that there are proven ways to do things – even if they are new to *you*. I can guarantee that for almost any goal you want to achieve, a successful road map or system has already been developed, and has been proven to work many times over. has been done before, and has been proven to work many times over.

There are astounding numbers of books and audio tapes that will expand your mind, help heal emotions, empower your spirit and boost your career, or help your search for your ideal profession. Read and listen to the information that will broaden your conciousness and impart wisdom to you that will be yours to keep forever.

Become a book and tape fiend and take in all the sage advice, wisdom, techniques, knowledge and know-how you possibly can absorb. The time it takes to read or listen will be nominal compared to all the knowledge you gain – remember, it stays with you forever! No time? Try to carve out just a sliver of your schedule, each day, for personal empowerment and professional growth.

Invest in audio tapes and turn your car into an advanced learning center – and turn wasted drive time into learning time. Practically any subject you can think of is already on cassette tape, so take advantage of it. Listen to audio tapes in the bath or shower, while shaving or putting on make up, and even while cooking. Buy a cassette player with earphones that you can take everywhere you go. Read for 15 minutes a night, right before you go to bed, and let positive motivational input be the last thing you experience before falling asleep. Set small goals you can easily keep and, again, build on your small successes.

I'd like to suggest a few specific books for general self-improvement and motivation. Many more are listed in the resource section at the back of this book. *Think and Grow Rich* By Napoleon Hill and *The Magic Of Thinking Big* by Dr. David Schwartz are phenomenal books. They provide clear-cut instructions on how to reach our goals and dreams. For the daily motivation we all need, I suggest reading the continuing series of *Chicken Soup For The Soul* books by Mark Victor Hansen and Jack Canfield. The 101 different uplifting stories in each book will provide you with daily inspiration. Andy Andrews' series of books, entitled *Storms Of Perfection*, will have the same uplifting results.

Make a list of all the topics that interest you: ways to make more money, start a business and/or develop relationship skills, and then take classes, seminars and seek out mentors. Find a way to get the information you want from the experts. Working hard is fine, but working smart is even better – and that means taking advantage of all the roadmaps already out there. Do whatever it takes to seek new horizons and educate yourself.

For continued success in the romantic arena, browse book stores and libraries in your home town, or places you visit; you can find endless books and audio tapes lining the store shelves and libraries every where. It's a small investment of money – and time – when you consider the benefits to your life.

A good sample includes: Gregory Godek's series of *1001 Ways To Be Romantic books*; Dr. Judy Kuriansky's *How To Love A Nice Guy*; Nachum Braverman & Shimon Apisdorf's *The Death Of Cupid*; and Gary Smalley's video series "Hidden Keys To Loving Relationships." Gary Chapman's book, *The Five Love Languages*, is also a great choice.

Maintaining a healthy sense of humor in all this is also important, whether you've already met your match or you're still looking. Both men and women will enjoy Sandra Beckwith's book *Why Can't A Man Be More Like A Woman?* It combines humor and keen insights in taking a lighthearted look at male behavior. Her bi-monthly newsletter, *The Do(o)Little Report*, is a riot.

As of this writing, there's a television show, *USA Live*, featuring Mayriah Moore, which gives dating tips and relationship advice every Friday afternoon on the USA Channel. Mayriah, known as "The Relationship Coach of The Nineties," is also author of *My, My, My...Dating In The Nineties*.

Those are just a few of my suggestions. There are hundreds more from which to choose. Get 'em, devour 'em and thrive. Remember, the roadmap is already out there. Seek it out.

Principle Number 2: *Apply the information immediately.*
Here's a fact, simply stated: "Knowledge without action is the same as not having any knowledge." To succeed in any quest you undertake you must take the information you've acquired and begin to apply it – immediately. Why? Because as human beings

we all have a tendency to put things off...wait until a better time...procrastinate. The longer the time between the time we learn something, and when we apply the knowledge, the greater the chances are we'll never get around to it.

Many people skim through a book such as this, get excited, tell themselves – and maybe all their friends – they are going to apply the information and yet, somehow, never get around to it. Even though they think of it often, something else always comes up, and they say things like, "One of these days I'm going to use that technique!" Unfortunately, they never do get around to doing it. I call those folks "as-soon-as people." They are people who are almost always in the "process" of getting ready to do something "as soon as"; for some of them, an entire lifetime flies by before they realize they never got around to taking the actions necessary to making their dreams come true.

I encourage you not to be one of those "as-soon-as" types.

Do a reality check on yourself. Have you heard yourself rationalizing with any of the following types of statements: "I'll start meeting some new people as soon as the busy season at work ends; I'll throw one of those parties I read about as soon as I lose this extra weight; as soon as I get some confidence in myself, I'll go to a Chamber of Commerce meeting and do some networking."

If you never quite "get around" to doing things, you can't develop confidence and fear maintains its presence in your life. We can all benefit by asking ourselves if, when we procrastinate, we are doing so out of fear. If so, there is a solution.

In his classic book *The Magic Of Thinking Big*, Dr. David Schwartz points out that *action cures fear*. The way to overcome a fear then, is to take action and *do what it is you fear*. And he's right. It works. I recommend doing it in small steps and, as always, building on your small successes.

For example, I used to have this incredible, almost sickening fear of calling women I didn't know very well to ask them out on a date. Whether this was due to fear of rejection or fear of saying the wrong thing...I don't know. It was fear – big time – and I hated it!

If I wanted to date the person badly enough, however, I'd force myself to call and ask. Sometimes the answer was "no," and sometimes "yes." Regardless what the answer was, the willingness to keep trying lessened my fear. The more calls I made, the more the fear went away. I expanded my comfort zone. In time, although my fear didn't completely disappear, it became practically nonexistent. The more action you take, the more you *can* take.

I cannot stress how important it is to jump-start your newfound knowledge into action, now. Go back to the beginning of this book, and read it (as well as other books you choose to learn from) over and over again until you get this system down. Allow yourself to absorb new ideas, while strengthening and internalizing new ones. Go ahead and mark up your books: Underline, highlight, make margin notes, star certain passages to your heart's content. Get busy! My advice to you is, after choosing the roadmaps to your goals and dreams, begin to follow them!

Principle Number 3: *Be Persistent*
Without persistence, there will be little success. Here's why: despite having a roadmap and putting it into immediate action, there will be setbacks. The bad news is, setbacks aren't fun. The good news is, with each setback we can become wiser, stronger, and more determined.

History is filled with the stories of famous men and women who struggled with and overcame numerous defeats before finally laying claim to ultimate personal victories. Many, in fact, that would eventually affect humankind. For instance, Henry Ford went bankrupt twice before starting Ford Motor Company; Colonel Sanders of Kentucky Fried Chicken fame heard "no" 1001 times before coming to the one "yes" that put his product on the market and changed the way this culture eats. Believe it or not, actress Sharon Stone was constantly turned down for roles in Hollywood because she was told she was *not sexy enough*! Books filled with these kinds of stories abound and are excellent reading for those times when we are tempted to wallow in our own self doubt. There are even more not-so-famous people who refused to stay down and who battled their way to victory.

We all get emotionally "knocked on our butts". Those who are determined to be winners simply refuse to stay there. They get back up. And what if they get knocked back down, again...and again? They get back up again...and again...and again! Each time they fall and pick themselves up they get stronger and stronger and more and more determined to reach their goal. It is from life's defeats and challenges that we all draw our greatest strengths.

I'd like to share with you a saying, in the form of a poem my Dad shared with me many years ago. I see this poem every day in my office and it serves as a reminder of what it takes to succeed. It reads as follows:

You are beaten to earth. Well, well, what's that?
Come up with a smiling face.
It's nothing against you to fall down flat,
but to lie there, that's disgrace.
The harder you're thrown, why, the higher you'll bounce.
Be proud of your blackened eye.
It isn't the fact that you're licked that counts.
It's how did you fight, and why?

What this poem says to me is that anyone, especially YOU can become a winner – a success in your business, social and romantic life! I guarantee it!

You've heard the saying, "Success is a journey, not a destination." How true. And the journey is a challenge. It is also a fact: Adjust your mindset so that you enjoy the journey and you'll continue to grow. So again, as a quick review of The Road Map to Success, seek out the information, apply it immediately, and be persistent!

I am rooting for you to enjoy an active dating life filled with nice, caring people, and/or to meet the mate of your dreams, and most definitely "live happily ever after." Keep working on yourself, as we all must, because the more emotionally fit you feel, the more emotionally fit the people you will attract into your life. I know it's going to happen for you.

Allow me to end with the entire text of a commencement address given by an aging Winston Churchill to a new crop of graduates from his college alma mater:

"Never give up. Never, never give up!"

Best of success always and in everything, especially ENDLESS ROMANCE!

GLOSSARY OF TERMS

Network Your Way To Endless Romance: A proven system that teaches people a step-by-step approach to developing an expansive network of people with whom mutually beneficial relationships can be developed. Next, consciously, and with great consideration, that network of people is enlisted to introduce quality men and women to one another; individuals who otherwise would not have had the chance to meet. The ultimate goal is to utilize this system to find "the mate of your dreams."

Networking: An arrangement of people crossed at regular intervals by other people, all of whom are cultivating mutually beneficial, give-and-take, win/win relationships with each other.

Romantic Resumé: A document that specifies the qualities you seek in the mate of your dreams and also describes who you are and the kind of relationship(s) you desire.

Referral-Based Dates: Dating opportunities that are facilitated and/or arranged by people in your network.

Proactive approach: When an individual takes an enthusiastic and active role in utilizing his or her network to meet the right person, enlisting networking friends to help search for potential dream mates and make introductions.

Reactive approach: When an individual chooses a more laid-back manner of searching for a mate, and enlists only certain networking friends to keep him or her in mind if they happen to come across an appropriate person.

Relationship Malpractice: A form of neglect and lack of communication in primary relationships that can result in emotional bankruptcy for a union if not remedied and paid proper care and attention.

High-volume conversations: One of the unfortunate results of lack of communication that can lead to Relationship Malpractice.

Sphere of Influence: The vast numbers of people who are in each individual's personal network. This includes all the individuals in any one person's professional and personal milieu.

Center of Influence: A person who is a highly respected, liked and trusted member of their profession, community and personal network. Centers of Influence are people who are widely recognized in their circles, and therefore excellent people with whom to network.

"You-oriented": A key style of communication that keeps the focus of a conversation on the "other," the person whom you want to know, like and trust you. An essential component of creating an expansive network.

"I-oriented": The style of communication many people engage in, mistakenly taking and bragging about themselves instead of allowing the person they want to impress to do most of the talking.

"You message": A style of communications in which the person speaking places blame and responsibility on others, as in "It's your fault!"; this generally produces negative results and incites defensive behaviors.

"I message": A way of taking full responsibility for your communication and presenting even the touchiest subjects in a positive light, so as to get a positive response.

Open-ended, Feel-good Questions: A positive and friendly method of asking questions designed to break the ice, keep people talking about themselves and make them feel good about themselves and the person who is asking them.

Extender Questions: Words and phrases that help to extend a conversation, keep it flowing and keep the other person engaged.

The Road Map To Success: The utilization of a compendium of proven formulas that help people expand their potential, and their lives, in and beyond the romantic arena

ABOUT THE *A*UTHORS

BOB BURG is internationally recognized as one of today's leading authorities on business networking. He is author of the highly acclaimed *ENDLESS REFERRALS: Network Your Everyday Contacts Into Sales* (McGraw-Hill, 1994) and the forthcoming *Winning Without Intimidation* (Samark Publishing, 1997).

A former television and radio personality, Bob is President of Burg Communications, Inc., in Jupiter, Florida and he presents keynote speeches and seminars internationally on the topic of business networking. He has shared the speaking platform with some of the world's most recognized speakers, including: Zig Ziglar, Larry King, Og Mandino, Willard Scott, Paul Harvey and former U.S. President Gerald Ford.

His unique experience as *COSMOPOLITAN* Magazine's "Bachelor of The Month" in 1994 was the inspiration for writing this book. His goal is to combine business networking skills with a search for romance that offers singles the best odds possible to meet the mate of their dreams.

LAURIE SUE BROCKWAY is recognized as a top reporter on relationships and sexuality. As former Editor-in-Chief of *PLAYGIRL* Magazine and author of several books on love and sex from the female point of view, she offers keen insights on finding romance in the nineties. She is known for a unique style of "participatory journalism," a method of becoming *part* of the stories she covers in order to gain *firsthand* experience. She is currently networking her way to endless romance!

Her work has appeared around the globe. For five years she syndicated her own work through her company *Star Reporter News Service*. She's also been syndicated by *Reuters, New York Times Syndicate, World Press Network and London Features*. Her articles have appeared in *NEW WOMAN, LADIES' HOME JOURNAL, WOMAN'S WORLD, MEN'S FITNESS, STAR* and *WOMAN'S OWN*; as well as the *New York Daily News, Newsday, Washington Post, Pittsburgh Press, Chicago Tribune, Chicago Sun Times, Miami Herald* and *Ft. Worth Star-Telegram*.

She's currently Editor-at-Large for both *PLAYGIRL* and the award winning *WOMEN'S NEWS*.

RESOURCE GUIDE

The following titles were researched and compiled by Cindy Dunn and several other kind, sharing people. They deal primarily with self-improvement, motivation, rapport building, and personal relationship building. It is suggested that you build a personal library of books and cassette tapes in order to fill your mind with the knowledge and good, positive thoughts that will help lead to your success.

Adams, Susan: *Marital Compatibility Test*. New York, NY, Carol Publishing, 1995.
Allan, Nick & Rosie: *101 Ways To Your Wife's/Husband's Heart*. New York, NY, Thomas Nelson, 1983.
Allen, Patricia: *Getting To I Do*. New York, NY, Avon, 1995.
Amodeo, John: *Being Intimate*. New York, NY, Penguin, 1988.
Amos, Wally "Famous Amos" & Gregory Amos: *The Power In You*. New York, NY, Donald I. Fine, Inc., 1988.
Andelin, Dr. Aubrey: *Men of Steel & Velvet*. Pierce City, MO, Pacific, 1990.
Andelin, Helen: *Fascinating Womanhood*. New York, NY, Bantam, 1992.
Andrews, Andy: *Storms of Perfection I*. Nashville, TN, Lighting Crown Publishers, 1992.
Andrews, Andy: *Storms of Perfection II*. Nashville, TN, Lighting Crown Publishers, 1994.
Andrews, Andy: *Storms of Perfection III*. Nashville, TN, Lighting Crown Publishers, 1996.
Andrews, Frank: *The Art & Practice of Loving*. New York, NY, Putnam, 1992.
Anthony, Dr. Robert B.: *The Ultimate Secrets of Total Self Confidence*. New York, NY, Berkley, 1987.
Arterburn, Stephen: *52 Simple Ways To Say I Love U*. Los Angeles, CA, Galahad, 1994.
Bailey, Lorilyn: *Original Lovers Questionnaire*. Login, 1994.
Barnett, Doyle: *20 Communication Tips for Couples*. Flushing, NY, New World, 1995.
Baron, Robert: *Are You My Type Am I Yours?* New York, NY, Harperco.

Barrows, Sydney Biddle: *Just Between Us Girls*. New York, NY, St. Martin's Press, 1996.
Beckwith, Sandra: *Why Can't A Man Be More Like A Woman?* New York, NY, Kensington Books, 1995.
Berne, Eric: *Games People Play*. New York, NY, Ballantine, 1985.
Bhaerman, Steve: *Friends & Lovers*. Boston, MA, Writers, 1986.
Biddle, J.: *214 Ways To Say I Love You*. Kensington.
Bloomfield, Harold: *Love Secrets For Lasting Relationships*. New York, NY, Bantam, 1994.
Branden, Nathaniel: *Psychology of Romantic Love*. New York, NY, 1985.
Branson, Ken: *Happy Together*. Portland, OR, Publisher, 1994.
Brasch, Rudy: *Book of Friendship*. New York, NY, Harperco, 1994.
Braverman, Nachum, and Shimon Apisdorf: *The Death of Cupid*. Baltimore, MD, Leviathan Press, 1996.
Breschi, Mike, Joe Preller, John Riggle: *Dating With Success*. Baltimore, MD, J.M.J. Publications, 1995.
Bristol, Claude M.: *The Magic of Believing*. New York, NY, Pocket, 1948.
Broder, Michael: *The Art of Staying Together*. New York, NY, 1994.
Brooks, Michael: *Instant Rapport*. New York, Warner Books, 1990.
Brothers, Dr. Joyce: *How To Get Whatever You Want Out of Life*. New York, NY, Ballantine, 1978.
Brothers, Dr. Joyce: *What Every Woman Should Know About Men*. New York, NY, Ballantine, 1987.
Brothers, Dr. Joyce: *What Every Woman Should Know About Love and Marriage*. New York, NY, Ballantine, 1985.
Burg, Bob: *Endless Referrals: Network Your Everyday Contacts Into Sales*. New York, NY, McGraw-Hill, 1994.
Buscaglia, Leo: *Born For Love*. New York, NY, Fawcett, 1994.
Buscaglia, Leo: *Love*. New York, NY, Fawcett, 1972.
Bushong, Carolyn: *Loving Him Without Losing You*. New York, NY, Berkley, 1993.
Cabot, Tracey: *Marrying Later Marrying Smart*. New York, NY, Dell.
Cain, Joella: *How To Figure Out Man / How To Figure Out Women*. Lower Lake, CA, Atrium-Cool Hand Comm., 1994.
Carlton, Ken: *What Men Want From Women*. New York, NY, Avon, 1995.
Carnegie, Dale: *How To Win Friends & Influence People*. New York, NY, Pocket Books, 1981.
Carnegie, Dale: *How to Stop Worrying & Start Living*. New York, NY, Pocket Books, 1984.
Carter, Steven: *He's Scared She's Scared*. New York, NY, Dell, 1995.

Carter, Steven: *Men Who Can't Love*. New York, NY, Berkley, 1988.
Chapin, Alice: *400 Creative Ways To Say I Love You*. Wheaton, IL, Tyndale, 1985.
Chapman, Gary: *The Five Love Languages*. Chicago, IL, Northfield, 1992.
Chapman, Gary: *Toward A Growing Marriage*. Chicago, IL, Moody, 1979.
Crowell, Al: *I'd Rather Be Married*. Oakland, CA, New Harbinger, 1995.
Crystal, Clarity: *Secrets of Love*. New York, NY, Warner.
Crystal, Clarity: *Secrets of Winning People*. New York, NY, Warner.
Cutler, W.: *Searching For Courtship*. New York, Random.
Cutter, Rebecca: *When Opposites Attract*. New York, NY, Viking, 1994.
David, B.: *Hugs & Kisses*. New York, NY, Workman.
Dayton, Tian: *Keeping Love Alive*. Deerfield Beach, FL, Health Comm., 1993.
DeAngelis, Barbara: *Are You The One For Me?* New York, NY, Doubleday, 1994.
DeAngelis, Barbara: *How To Make Love All The Time*. New York, NY, Dell, 1991.
DeAngelis, Barbara: *Real Moments*. New York, NY, Doubleday, 1995.
DeAngelis, Barbara: *Secrets About Men Every Woman*. New York, NY, Dell.
DeAngelis, Barbara: *Real Moments For Lovers*. New York, NY, Delacorte, 1995.
DeAngelis, Barbara: *Confidence: Finding It & Living It*. Carson, CA, Hay House, 1995.
Derman, Bruce: *We'd Have A Great Relationship If*. Deerfield Beach, FL, Health Comm., 1994.
Dominitz, Ben: *How To Find the Love of Your Life*. Rocklin, CA, Prima, 1993.
Donovan, M.: *Love Blocks*. New York, NY, Penguin.
Dreyfus, Edward A.: *Someone Right For You*. New York, NY, McGraw, 1992.
Driscoll, Richard: *Recovering Love*. New York, NY, Simon & Schuster, 1993.
Drury, M.: *Advice To Young Wife From Old*. New York, NY, Random, 1995.
Edmark, Tomima: *365 Ways To Kiss Your Love*. Summit, TX, Summit Group, 1993.
Edwards, Susan: *When Men Believe In Love*. New York, NY, Penguin, 1995.
Elgin, Suzette H.: *Genderspeak*. New York, NY, John Wiley & Sons, 1993.
Ellenberg, Daniel: *Lovers For Life*. Livingston, NJ, Asian Publishers, 1995.
Emmons, Michael: *Accepting Each Other*. Greenwich, CT, Impact, 1991.
Fast, Julius: *Body Language*. New York, NY, Pocket Books, 1970.
Fay, Allen: *PQR Prescription For Quality Relationship*. Kirkwood, MO, Impact, 1994.
Fein, Ellen: *Rules*. New York, NY, Warner, 1994.
Fincham, Frank: *Communicating in Relationships*. Washington D.C., Research, 1993.
Fincham, Frank: *The Psychology of Marriage*. New York, NY, Guilford Press, 1990.
Francis, Cindy: *Life Lessons For Couples*. Golden, CO, Andrews, 1995.

Frankel, V.: *Heartbreak Handbook*. New York, NY, Fawcett, 1993.
Gabor, Don: *How To Talk To People You Love*. New York, NY, Simon & Schuster, 1989.
Giblin, Les: *How To Have Confidence And Power In Dealing With People*. Englewood Cliffs, NJ, Prentice-Hall, 1956.
Godek, Gregory J.P.: *1001 Ways To Be Romantic*. Weymouth, MA, Casablanca Press, 1991.
Godek, Gregory J.P.: *1001 More Ways To Be Romantic*. Weymouth, MA, Casablanca Press, 1992.
Godek, Gregory J.P.: *Romance 101 Lessons In Love*. Weymouth, MA, Casablanca Press, 1993.
Godek, Gregory J.P.: *The Portable Romantic*. Weymouth, MA, Casablanca Press, 1994.
Godek, Gregory J.P.: *The Lover's Bedside Companion*. Weymouth, MA, Casablanca Press, 1994.
Gray, John: *Men Are From Mars, Women Are From Venus*. New York, NY, Harper Collins, 1995.
Gray, John: *Mars & Venus In The Bedroom*. New York, NY, Harper Collins, 1995.
Gray, John: *Men, Women & Relationships: Making Peace with Opposite Sex*. St. Paul, MN, Beyond Works, 1990.
Gray, John: *What Your Mother Couldn't Tell You & Your Father Didn't Know: Advanced Relationship Skills for Lasting Intimacy*. New York, NY, HarperCo., 1994.
Gray, John: *What You Feel You Can Heal: A Guide for Enriching Relationships*. Los Angeles, CA, Heart Pub., 1994.
Hanson, Mark Victor, and Jack Canfield: *Chicken Soup for the Soul*. Deerfield Beach, FL, 1993.
Hanson, Mark Victor, and Jack Canfield: *A Second Helping of Chicken Soup for the Soul*. Deerfield Beach, FL, 1995.
Harley, Willard F.: *His Needs, Her Needs, Building An Affair Proof Marriage*. Old Tappan, NJ, Revell, 1986.
Harris, Amy Bjork, and Thomas A. Harris: *Staying OK*. New York, NY, Avon, 1986.
Harris, Thomas A.: *I'm OK-You're OK*. New York, NY, Avon, 1976
Hill, Napoleon & W. Clement Stone: *Success Through A Positive Mental Attitude*. New York, NY, Pocket Books, 1960.
Hill, Napoleon: *Think And Grow Rich*. New York, NY, Fawcett Publications, 1987.
Hocking, David: *Love & Marriage*. Eugene, OR, Harvest House, 1981.
Jeffers, Susan: *Feal The Fear and Do It Anyway*. New York, NY, Ballentine

Books, 1988.

Kent, Margaret: *How To Marry The Man Of Your Choice*. New York, NY, Warner, 1987.

King, Larry: *How To Talk To Anyone, Anytime, Anywhere*. New York, NY, Crown Publishers, Inc., 1994.

Kipfer, Barbara: *Bartlett's Book Of Love Quotations*. New York, NY, Little & Brown, 1994.

Kipfer, Barbara: *14,000 Things To Be Happy About*. New York, NY, Workman, 1990.

Kriedman, Ellen: *Light His Fire*. New York, NY, Dell, 1989.

Kriedman, Ellen: *Light Her Fire*. New York, NY, Dell, 1989.

Kyne, Peter D.: *The Go-Getter*. New York, NY, Henry Holt & Company, Inc., 1949.

LaHaye, Tim & Beverly: *The Act of Marriage*. New York, NY, Bantam, 1976.

Lerner, Ph.D., Harriet G.: *The Dance of Intimacy, A Woman's Guide To Courageous Acts of Change in Key Relationships*. New York, NY, Harper & Row, 1989.

Littauer, Florence: *Personality Plus*. Old Tappan, NJ, Revell, 1983.

Littauer, Florence: *After Every Wedding Comes A Marriage*. Eugene, OR, Harvest House, 1981.

Littauer, Florence: *Silver Boxes*. Dallas, TX, Word, 1989.

Lontos, Pam: *Don't Tell Me It's Impossible Until After I've Already Done It*. New York, NY, William Morrow, 1986.

Lovric, Michelle: *Love Letters*. New York, NY, Shooting Star Press, 1994.

Maltz, Maxwell: *PsychoCybernetics*. North Hollywood, CA, Wilshire Books, 1973.

Moore, Mayriah: *My, My, My...Dating in the 90's, Your Personal Pocket Guide to Dating*. New York, NY, Mapp Publishing, 1995.

McGinnis, Alan Loy: *The Friendship Factor*. Minneapolis, MN, Augsburg Press, 1979.

McGinnis, Alan Loy: *The Romance Factor*. New York, NY, Harper & Row, 1982.

McGinnis, Alan Loy: *Bring Out The Best In People*. Minneapolis, MN, Augsburg Press, 1985.

McInnes-Smith, Lisa & Daniel Johnson & Winston Marsh: *How To Motivate, Manage & Market Yourself*. Mulgrave, Vic., McPherson's Printing Group, 1989.

Newman, Bill: *Soaring With Eagles*. Toowomg, QLD, Australia, 1994.

Peale, Norman Vincent: *The Power of Positive Thinking*. New York, NY, Ballantine, 1991.

Peale, Norman Vincent: *The Tough Minded Optimist*. New York, NY, Ballantine, 1961.

Qubein, Nido R.: *Communicate Like A Pro*. New York, NY, Berkley, 1983.

Robbins, Anthony: *Personal Power*. New York, NY, Fawcett, 1987.
Robbins, Anthony: *Awaken The Giant Within*. New York, NY, Simon & Schuster, 1992.
Robbins, Anthony: *Giant Steps*. New York, NY, Simon & Schuster, 1994.
Ross, Randal: *7 Habits of Winning Relationships*. Tulsa, OK, Viacom, Inc., 1992.
Schuller, Robert H.: *Tough Times Never Last But Tough People Do!* New York, NY, Bantam, 1983.
Schuller, Robert H.: *Move Ahead with Possibility Thinking*. Old Tappan, NJ, Revell, 1967.
Schuller, Robert H.: *You Can Become The Person You Want To Be*. New York, NY, Hawthorne Books, 1973.
Schwartz, David: *The Magic of Thinking Big*. New York, NY, Simon & Schuster, 1987.
Shedd, Charlie: *Letters To Karen*. New York, NY, Avon, 1965.
Shedd, Charlie: *Letters To Phillip*. New York, NY, Jove, 1978.
Smalley, Gary, and John Trent: *Love Is A Decision*. Dallas, TX, Word, 1987.
Smalley, Gary: *The Language of Love*. Dallas, TX, Word, 1987.
Stoddard, Alexandra: *Living A Beautiful Life*. New York, NY, Avon, 1991.
Stoddard, Alexandra: *Living Beautifully Together*. New York, NY, Avon, 1989.
Stoddard, Alexandra: *Daring To Be Yourself*. New York, NY, Avon, 1990.
Stoddard, Alexandra: *The Gift of a Letter*. New York, NY, Avon, 1990.
Stoddard, Alexandra: *Making Choices*. New York, NY, William Morrow, 1994.
Stoddard, Alexandra: *The Art of the Possible*. New York, NY, William Morrow, 1993.
Stoddard, Alexandra: *Grace Notes*. New York, NY, William Morrow, 1993.
Swindoll, Charles R.: *Dropping Your Guard, The Value of Open Relationships*. New York, NY, Bantam, 1983.
Tannen, Deborah: *You Just Don't Understand*. New York, NY, William Morrow, 1990.
The Best of Bits & Pieces. Fairfield, NJ, The Economic Press, Inc., 1994.
Vaughn, Gabriel H.: *Shining Your Armour, For Married Men Only: The Lost Art of Romance*. Orlando, FL, Shining Your Armour Publishing, 1990.
Waitley, Denis: *The Psychology of Winning*. New York, NY, Berkley Books, 1984.
Waitley, Denis: *Seeds of Greatness*. New York, NY, Pocket, 1983.
Wright, H. Norman: *How To Get Along With Almost Anyone*. Dallas, TX, Word, 1989.
Ziglar, Zig: *Courtship After Marriage*. Thomas Nelson, Nashville, TN, 1990.

INDEX